# YOU ARE BEING WATCHED

---

**A layperson's guide to protecting your digital lifestyle**

---

**Alvin Rodrigues**

Given the many publications on the topic, I was initially sceptical when Alvin mentioned his intention to write a cybersecurity book. Many either delve too much into the technicalities, deterring readers, or present outdated information by the time of publication. Others, while trying to be clear, end up feeling like forgettable textbooks. However, after previewing Alvin's book, I was relieved that his is different.

He cleverly utilises fictional characters to explain the significance of cybersecurity in relatable day-to-day conversations. The story serves as a cautionary tale, highlighting the vulnerabilities we all share.

I like that the "Over to You" section engages readers to contemplate their actions in similar scenarios. The book encourages readers to critically evaluate their online habits and adopt timeless cybersecurity principles, from protecting access to their accounts and digital assets, reducing their attack surface, and avoiding the pitfalls and traps laid out by cybercriminals on the Internet.

Last but not least, these cybersecurity insights are pertinent to everyone, from students to CEOs.

I hope you enjoy the book as much as I did.

By William Tam,
Head of Telstra Purple Technical Consulting, North Asia, Telstra Purple

This new book by seasoned cybersecurity practitioner and first-time author Alvin Rodrigues is a refreshing take on cybersecurity awareness and hygiene and how a blatant disregard for it will impact the digital lifestyle of the person in the street. The book aims to provide the reader with valuable insights and guidance on how to improve his or her personal cybersecurity posture. To achieve this, the various cybersecurity concepts were organised into "four mindset shifts", and "four pillars of protection" and explained through the dialogue between a dating couple, James and his cybersecurity consultant girlfriend, Amber, over a course of 3½ days. James started as a skeptic but, through being more informed by Amber, ended off as a believer, eventually convinced that it is better to be proactively cybersecurity-savvy rather than be on the receiving end of a cybersecurity breach.

The author creatively employs analogies such as breadcrumbs (traces of online activities), castle (devices), jewels (data and information), rogue courier (man-in-the-middle attack), castle's gate (router), poisoned goods (malicious advertisements), plug-in (armour), credential sniffing (pickpocket stealing the castle's keys), garage (own computer), application (car), unlocked car (not logging out) to illustrate technical terms, presumably to make reading more understandable and fun!

There are lots of useful references for the reader, such as the 13 appendices, which are a convenient compilation of must-know topics and useful tips such as "What are lookalike domains, and how to avoid them?", "Password checklist", "Checklist for phishing scam", "Individual Breach Recovery Plan", "Social media account recovery". I personally find them a good back-to-basics refresher, but you may choose to ignore them if you are an advanced reader or at your own peril.

Finally, in my opinion, this is a much-needed book to bring a beginner up to speed on cyber hygiene with the technical jargon creatively illustrated in a layperson's language. I commend Alvin Rodrigues for his vision and tenacity to devote his personal time and money to bring cyber hygiene education to the man in the street.

By Alvin Ong, Chief Information Officer, NTU Singapore

A truly heart-to-heart talk on cybersecurity, "You Are Being Watched" takes a fresh look at cyber essentials and weaves them into a couple's conversation in the author's personal style of storytelling. This modern-day love story shares some practical tips on how to secure our valuable data in our daily digital lives. It offers a new and interesting way to learn cybersecurity concepts using easy-to-understand language with down-to-earth examples you can share with family and friends.

By Paolo Miranda<br>Vice President of (ISC)2 Singapore Chapter

A systematic and informative read that every digital citizen needs. It illuminates many hidden risks forged by mindsets of ignorance and habits of convenience. To continue to harness the best of the digital environment and technologies, we need to strengthen digital citizenry and this book accomplishes exactly that.

By YEO Chuen Chuen, Managing Director, ACESENCE Agile<br>Leadership, Author of Leaders People Love

My son's Roblox account was compromised, and he shouted, "Why would anyone do that to me?". I wish I had Alvin's "You Are Being Watched" book handy, which would take him on an educational odyssey through the character of James. He faces the alarming reality of cybersecurity vulnerabilities following an unsettling incident.

The book provides answers through the lens of Amber, James' tech-savvy partner, who helps demystify essential cybersecurity practices in an easily digestible format. The storytelling approach keeps the material engaging and makes the complex world of cybersecurity relatable and understandable.

This book uniquely combines a compelling narrative with practical, real-world advice, making it accessible to people from all walks of life. Comprehensive yet easy to read, it's an indispensable resource for anyone aiming to safeguard their digital lifestyle.

Leonard Ong
ISACA Singapore Chapter President, 2012-2014
ISACA International Board of Directors, 2015-2019

In the past, I believed cybersecurity was the concern of only companies and government agencies. Yet, after reading this insightful book, I've changed my perspective. Given my numerous hours online, sharing personal moments, and handling sensitive transactions, my personal information is at risk of being stolen.

My details are alarmingly vulnerable; I risk losing access to my accounts, having my social identity hijacked, and even having my money stolen. It's evident from the news that such incidents are becoming increasingly commonplace. While I don't make a living online, those who do are at greater risk of their livelihoods being threatened.

Loads of people need to have cybersecurity literacy because so much is at stake. This book does an excellent job of spelling out just what you and I, as non-technical individuals, could stand to lose. The author uses analogies and metaphors, making it easier for us to make sense of the more complex and technical concepts.

I know learning cybersecurity can sometimes be a drag, especially if your company makes you do it (though, really, think about why they're putting so much into it: because they need you to be on defence). But this book makes it easy to digest and, dare I say it, fun!

By She-reen Wong<br>Non-technical Reader

"You Are Being Watched" is the ultimate cyber adventure for today's savvy generation. James and Amber's journey is an electrifying tale of digital dangers, seamlessly interwoven with vital cybersecurity lessons into a thrilling narrative. In particular, Amber, as the tech-savvy heroine, serves to inspire more young women to enter this highly male-dominated space! An indispensable guide for millennials, "You Are Being Watched" is a practical read but a must for anyone seeking a fun and secure digital journey.

By Mabel Loh,<br>AMFIT Founder and Principal Trainer of AMFIT

Alvin's concoction of romance, intrigue, and online protection is genre-bending and unique. I never thought it was possible to blend everything together so artfully for an engaging and practical read.

I highly recommend all corporate and individual online users to go through the book and keep the checklist that comes with it handy.

Having your accounts breached and data or money stolen is an ordeal you will never want to live through. You can minimise the chances of this happening to you, and there's no better place to start than this book.

By Danny Lim, Director, IN.FOM

This remarkable book has been an eye-opener for me. It unveils a multitude of strategies to fortify our accounts against potential hackers. If you believe losing a social media account is the gravest threat, think again.

The prospect of identity theft looms, where malefactors could mimic you so convincingly that even your nearest and dearest could fall prey to scams.

The book is a breeze to read, and most crucially, it empowers you with actionable steps to establish robust defences on your own terms. I've already implemented some of the recommendations—have you?

Rayn Lim, Forex Coach

## *Disclaimer*

This book has been written to provide information about You Are Being Watched: A Layperson's Guide to Protecting Your Digital Lifestyle. Every effort has been made to make this book as complete and accurate as possible.

However, there may be mistakes in typography or content. Also, this book provides information only up to the publishing date. Therefore, this book should be used as a guide - not as the ultimate source.

The purpose of this book is to educate. The author and the publisher do not warrant that the information contained in this book is fully complete and shall not be responsible for any errors or omissions. The author and publisher shall have neither liability nor responsibility to any person or entity with respect to any loss or damage caused or alleged to be caused directly or indirectly by this book.

## *Acknowledgement*

I want to thank those who contacted me for help during their security breaches. The experiences we shared, the lessons we learned, and the journey we embarked on together were instrumental in shaping this book's concepts, structure, thought processes, and overall flow.

I'd like to express my heartfelt appreciation to all my reviewers for their invaluable feedback. Your comments have been instrumental in maintaining the clarity and readability of the content, enhancing comprehension through metaphors and analogies, effectively conveying the desired objectives, and refining the language and writing style. Your input has greatly contributed to the overall quality of the work.

Alvin Ong, Danny Lim, Ganesh Vikram, Leonard Ong, Mabel Loh, Manish Bansal, Paolo Miranda, Raju Chellam, Rayn Lim, She-reen Wong, William Tam and Yeo Chuen Chuen.

I would also like to express my gratitude to Theresa Lin for her imaginative illustrations, which have contributed to making the technical subject of cybersecurity more friendly and palatable.

Finally, I must extend my profound appreciation to my wife, Ai Ling, whose unwavering support has been nothing short of remarkable. She has not only shouldered the responsibilities of caring for our children but graciously afforded me the necessary time to work on this project. Her provision of snacks and late-night cups of hot tea when I am deeply engrossed in my writing, has been a sustaining force that keeps me energised and focused.

# Table of Contents

*This page was intentionally left blank.*

# Introduction

In today's interconnected world, the prevalence of cyberattacks on individuals has risen dramatically. As digital engagement increases, so does our vulnerability to cyber threats. Cybercriminals have become more sophisticated, exploiting the naive and the unprepared with tactics that range from phishing scams to ransomware attacks.

I remember one case where an individual experienced a cyberextortion scam. She usually watches YouTube and TikTok mounted in a waterproof holder in her shower. One day, she received an email informing her that the cybercriminal had embarrassing photographs and videos of her and threatened to expose them unless she paid the demanded ransom. The cybercriminal also claimed to have access to her bank accounts. She contacted me in a panic-stricken state. While we worked together and managed to overcome her situation, that day was the longest day of her life, fearing for her assets, reputation, and future.

These intrusions are not only distressing, causing panic, but they can also lead to significant financial and personal losses. The advent of the digital age has undoubtedly brought convenience and innovation. Yet, it also necessitates increased vigilance and robust security measures to counter these pervasive threats.

*Welcome to You Are Being Watched*

This book is designed to provide you with valuable insights and guidance on how to improve your personal cybersecurity posture.

It targets individuals between 18 and 40 but does not exclude those who are frequently online outside of this age group. It is about cybersecurity for the everyday individual, "the person on the street", by providing a greater appreciation and realisation of the importance of cybersecurity in this digital era. It also offers mindset shifts to improve your security posture by inculcating cyber security as an everyday habit that directly benefits you, and indirectly your family, loved ones, and friends.

This book offers many tips, recommendations, and advice to minimise cyber-attack risks as you explore and navigate the digital world. This is akin to The Highway Code that promotes road user safety or "Internet User Safety" as you travel on the "Information Super-Highway."

This book addresses a glaring need for contextualised materials that bridge the gap between the why, what, and how of cybersecurity for individuals. Although its primary emphasis is on individual learning, it also serves as a base for encouraging individuals to explore deeper into cybersecurity, thereby extending their knowledge and practices into organisational settings. Instead of being the vulnerable point in the security structure, individuals can transform into the most robust link, creating a human firewall that strengthens our cybersecurity framework. This book nurtures the growth of this human firewall one person at a time, turning potential weaknesses into an empowering defence.

To achieve this, cybersecurity must be presented in an accessible and understandable manner, ensuring that concepts, strategies, and ideas can be readily applied to everyone's unique circumstances, rendering them real and effective.

To make the most of this book, immerse yourself in the story and enjoy the three and a half days' worth of conversations between Amber, a cybersecurity consultant in her early 30s and her boyfriend, James, also in his early 30s. He is an up-and-coming social media influencer who has experienced a breach that locked him out of his social media platforms.

The conversation between Amber and James is enriched with analogies and everyday metaphor. Footnotes direct you to an appendix section where you find personal security posture assessment questions, quick reference guides, checklist, to do list, and even a personal breach recovery plan that Amber used on James and more. These tools will bolster your security stance and cyber hygiene, lessening your cyberattack vulnerability.

***The book is divided into three parts.***

The first part introduces four mindset shifts crucial for personal change and conviction. It also focuses on self-assessment, self-discovery, self-awareness, and self-realisation, providing a baseline for improvement. You will uncover your digital assets and how you manage them, learn the risk behind online habits and the digital breadcrumbs you leave behind, discover your risk appetite, and grasp the motivations of cybercriminals and the specific threats you, as an individual, are exposed to.

Within the book's second section lies a comprehensive exploration of the four pillars of protection, presenting you with a strategic framework to safeguard yourself effectively. The initial three pillars concentrate on fortifying your digital environment (your digital home or castle) against cyberattacks, analogous to reinforcing the security of your physical house against unwanted intruders.

The fourth pillar examines your online behaviour and habits beyond the boundaries of your digital haven. It equips you with the knowledge and techniques to navigate the Internet safely, avoiding potential traps and pitfalls set by cybercriminals. Additionally, it emphasises the importance of cultivating simple yet powerful habits that enhance your overall security posture. By following these guidelines, you can bolster your defences and minimise the risks associated with cyber threats.

The last part of the book emphasises the importance of staying relevant in the ever-evolving landscape of cybersecurity.

Despite technology's ever-changing nature, the fundamental process of connecting to the Internet remains consistent, involving three essential steps: device connection, network connection, and Internet access. Consequently, this served as the guiding principle for assembling the four pillars discussed in the book's second part. The foundational knowledge gained in identifying vulnerabilities, overcoming them, and safeguarding yourself remains pertinent as long as the unaltered three-step Internet connection process persists.

This book intends to help you towards a more secure online presence, embrace the knowledge within these pages, and may your newfound understanding empower you to explore and navigate the digital world with confidence and resilience.

# Chapter One

## The Breach

*James' Digital World Crumbles Before Him*

In the realm of social media influencers, there was no one quite like James. He is an up-and-coming social media influencer with a vibrant personality and an uncanny knack for generating content, and he has amassed a large following. He was a fixture in the travel and lifestyle space, providing his audience with reviews of picturesque travel locations and tantalising dining experiences. His pictures were perfect, his videos were enthralling, and his commentary was captivating.

However, despite being a digital native and a social media savant, James was not security-savvy. Like many in his generation, he understood the potential dangers of the cyber world, yet he largely dismissed them. He perceived cybersecurity as a cumbersome hurdle, an annoyance that only stood in the way of him sharing his next great adventure with his followers.

Amber, James' girlfriend, was the antithesis of James when it came to technology. As a cybersecurity consultant, she was acutely aware of the ever-present threat of digital invaders. She advised him regularly about proper cyber hygiene, but her words were brushed aside. James, stubborn and set in his ways, had this erroneous belief that he was too insignificant and had nothing of value to be a target of a cyberattack.

Then came the day that changed everything.

An email dropped into James' inbox, supposedly from a company that wished to sponsor his upcoming travel to a new resort in Japan. The opportunity was enticing, filled with all the promise of new content for his followers and a potential boost for his online persona. He immediately clicked on the link, filled out a form with his details, and downloaded what he thought was a briefing document.

But lurking beneath the surface was a threat that he had always underestimated.

Without realising it, he had fallen prey to a classic cyber-attack. The downloaded document had released malware into his computer, an invisible saboteur that sought his login credentials. A carefully replicated fake social media website also lured him into inputting his username and password, which the hackers promptly stole.

James discovered his digital disaster when he tried to log into his social media account and found himself locked out. His credentials were no longer valid, and the reset password link was sent to an unknown email. Panic set in. His source of income, connection to his followers, and identity were all instantly stolen.

Frantic, he called Amber, confessing to his disastrous situation. His voice trembled as he admitted to using the same password for all his social media accounts, and a chilling realisation set in. Already fearing the worst, Amber instantly instructed him to check his other social media accounts while on the call with him. The hacker had discovered this pattern and methodically locked him out of all his accounts. His breath hitched as he found each of them inaccessible, his worst fears confirmed. Horrified but not surprised, Amber immediately relayed to her manager that she was dealing with a personal emergency and hastily left the office to be by his side. Her worst predictions about James' cyber hygiene materialised into a horrifying reality.

### *Over To You*

As a reader, you can't help but feel empathy for James, a young man who just saw his world crumble around him. But the incident also begs reflection on your cyber hygiene. Are you, like James, underestimating the threats that exist in the digital realm? Do you take cybersecurity seriously or consider it an inconvenient additional step in your digital life?

In the next chapter, you can expect to see more details about your cybersecurity training with Amber as you start your self-awareness and discovery journey. There will likely be some struggles as you work to change your mindset and habits, but the chapter will guide your progress and growth.

# CHAPTER TWO

## A Cyber Wake-up Call

*James' Journey of Self-Discovery, Awareness and Realisation*

James was in a state of denial. When Amber found him at home, he was distraught, battling waves of frustration and misery. The question, "Why me?" echoed persistently in his mind. In the grand scheme of the digital universe, he considered himself a small fish. Why would cyber criminals target him? All he had was his social media - his lifeline, his income. He saw himself as a nobody compared to the illustrious social media superstars. "Why me?"

Amber, the pillar of support, walked into the bedroom and enfolded him in a comforting embrace. She swallowed her urge to say, "I told you so." Now was not the time to rub salt into his fresh wounds. Sensing his vulnerability, she carried herself carefully, reminding herself of the fine line between pushing him further into despair and coaxing him towards enlightenment about his lax attitude towards cybersecurity.

Mustering her courage, she broached the subject of account recovery. Her voice softened as she admitted that retrieving his accounts would be arduous, inconvenient, emotionally taxing, and there are no assurances. If their efforts proved futile, he would face the devastating loss of his meticulously crafted online identity, built painstakingly over the years.

Feeling the weight of their task, Amber decided it was time to evaluate James' cybersecurity awareness and hygiene. She had her assumptions but needed confirmation. With a tact only a loving partner could muster, she gently questioned him about his security measures, mindful not to push him further into his defensive shell. This conversation, she knew, was as much about recovering his accounts as it was about instigating a change in his mindset towards cybersecurity.

That Friday afternoon, they spent hours contacting family, loved ones, friends, his social media community followers, and corporate clients to inform them that all his social media accounts were compromised. Amber began monitoring James's social media accounts to watch for any suspicious or reputation-harming actions by the hijackers. James also reported to the social media platforms that his accounts were hijacked. They also requested friends, loved ones, and some close followers write on their behalf about the account compromise. Amber reassured James that they were doing everything possible to recover his accounts, and that he had to be patient and ready with proof that the hijacked accounts were his.

Amber probed his security protocols: his approach to safeguarding his devices and networks, password management, data privacy, and overall online behaviour. She aimed to assess his current status and help him understand the scope of his shortcomings.[1]

The conclusion was unsurprising but disheartening: James had abysmal cyber hygiene. Amber realised that even if they managed to regain control of his accounts, he was bound to make the same mistakes without a change in his attitude and online behaviour. She started to consider a personalised cybersecurity awareness programme for him. She loves him and believes he must learn to fend for himself in this increasingly digitalised world.

Amber drew from an adage: "Give a man a fish, and you feed him for a day; teach a man to fish, and you feed him for a lifetime." She desired James to recognise cyber threats independently and make informed decisions about his online activities. After all, his online brand 'James' was not just important to him. It was crucial to their shared future. Little did James know his journey was beginning.

### *James' cyber self-awareness and change journey begins*

Amber began the conversation by gently managing James' expectations. She warned him that their approach would be meticulous and might take longer than he'd prefer but assured him that it was vital to be thorough. She presented him with a list of elements that she felt were key to understanding his current and much-needed desired cybersecurity posture.

- Four mindsets, catalyst for change.

---

[1] Go to Appendix 01. Questions Amber used to examine James' security posture – A Personal Security Posture Assessment.

- James' digital assets and how he manages them.
- James in his digital realm - reasons, connection, habits, and breadcrumbs.
- James' risk appetite.
- Know thy cybercriminals.
- Threats targeting individuals.

James was overwhelmed, but he listened, a silent acknowledgement that he was at the starting line of his cybersecurity journey.

### *Coaching to Consciousness*

Amber initiated her guidance by drawing from two fundamental statements: "By failing to prepare, you are preparing to fail" and "Begin with the end in mind". She knew that his meticulous planning and execution of his social media content were his strengths. So, she encouraged him to apply the same strategy to his cybersecurity learning journey.

Amber guided him gently and asked him to consider his valuable assets, those he wanted to protect and his reasons for doing so. What were the consequences if these assets were compromised? She asked him to reflect on his online habits, questioning their safety and whether his actions risked his assets.

James became defensive. He bristled at Amber's prodding, expressing his irritation and uncertainty about the relevance of these questions. His sole interest was to recover his accounts and continue his life. This reaction was a red flag to Amber, indicating that without a shift in his mindset, he might revert to his old habits once his accounts were restored.

Amber reminded James that he had to be patient and wait for the platform providers to respond as they continued working on recovering his account. She highlights that this entire learning journey is part of account recovery and preventing being compromised again.

Amber continued tactfully and patiently, steering the conversation towards the broader picture. She emphasised the importance of becoming cybersecurity-savvy, understanding his vulnerabilities, and not repeating the same mistakes. She nudged him to consider his cybersecurity journey a continuous learning process, starting with the end goal: of minimising his risk of future compromises.

She shared an analogy: she wanted James to build his cybersecurity knowledge like a house of bricks, not straw or wood, so that when the 'big bad' cybercriminals come knocking again, his defences would withstand their attacks.

After much persuasion, James very reluctantly agreed to invest his time and effort in learning to defend himself against future cyber threats. This agreement began his long-overdue transformation from a digital native to a cybersecurity-aware netizen.

### *Mindsets: The Invisible Drivers of Change*

Amber had ignited a glimmer of interest within James, who, although initially resistant, was now on the cusp of embracing a critical journey towards cybersecurity literacy. With her empathetic yet firm approach, she took the opportunity to delicately unravel the fabric of the four key mindsets, in numerical order, that lay at the heart of this transformation.

### *Mindset #1*

> *"Your data, accounts and credentials are valuable to cybercriminals"*

Amber explained that his personal information, such as full name, date of birth, identity card number, passport, bank account information and more, while seemingly ordinary, could be a treasure trove for cybercriminals. To illustrate, she mentioned the potential consequences of identity theft, monetary fraud, and social sabotage. James found himself caught between scepticism and intrigue. Though he respected Amber and her expertise, he struggled to fully accept that his ordinary personal data could be a target for cybercriminals.

The thought of his daily online interactions being scrutinised and valued by cybercriminals, let alone used for malicious intents, was difficult for him to fathom. However, he couldn't deny the logic behind Amber's words. The possibilities of identity theft, financial fraud, and social defamation were too real.

His mind began to wander, churning with a swirl of thoughts. Could his recent breach have been avoided if he'd placed more value on his digital assets? Would he have been more diligent, more protective? Would he have paid more attention to the precautions he'd often dismissed as needless? The questions kept flooding in, each gnawing at his disbelief and propelling him toward an understanding he was not ready to embrace fully.

James chose to listen, not interrupting Amber's passionate discourse. He appreciated her efforts and desired to help him navigate the complex cybersecurity web. Even though he was still wrestling with doubt, he couldn't dismiss the nagging feeling that Amber was on to something important that could change his entire approach to his online presence.

So, he continued to listen, silently wrestling with the implications of this newfound perspective. He was far from convinced, yet he couldn't shake off the creeping realisation that his understanding of cybersecurity was about to take a radical turn.

## _Over To You_

While you're reading this, take a moment to think about the essence of your digital assets. Your personal and financial information, online engagements, and choices paint a picture of your digital existence. Do you realise the potential worth of this picture to cyber attackers?


### *Mindset #2*

*"Cybersecurity is not too complex, technical, or difficult for you"*

Amber leaned forward, eager to address the misconception that cybersecurity is overly complex, technical, and difficult. "James, now that you know that you have assets of value to the cybercriminals, what are you prepared to do to protect yourself? For you to successfully protect yourself, you need to become cybersecurity savvy. Here is where I would like you to shift away from the mindset that cybersecurity is too complex, technical and difficult to learn."

She paused momentarily, thinking about a suitable analogy before continuing, "Imagine you want to lock your front door. Do you need to be a locksmith to know how to do it?" Answering her question, she said, "Of course not! You only need to know what lock you want, how to use the lock, when to use a single or double-bolt lock, and whether to install a peephole on the door or even a gate with a lock to enhance your security. It's about taking everyday actions to secure your home."

James nodded, following along with the analogy. "So, you're saying that cybersecurity is similar? It's about selecting the right security solutions, adopting good everyday cyber habits and practices to protect my digital life without needing to be a technical expert."

Amber exclaimed. "Exactly! It is about being secure. It is about being mindful and aware of your online activities, using strong passwords, being cautious of suspicious emails, links, or file attachments, keeping your device operating systems and apps updated and more.

James smiled, starting to grasp the concept. "I see now. Just like I don't need to be a locksmith to lock my doors, I don't need to be a technical cybersecurity professional to practice good cybersecurity. Hence, learning appropriate and relevant areas of cyber security to be secure should not be that complex, technical or difficult to learn."

Amber nodded enthusiastically. "That's right! As we continue the discussion, you will realise that cyber security is part security solutions, part rolling out security solutions aligned to how you behave in the digital world and part about your awareness, digital attitudes, and habits. And we are continuously adjusting these three areas to achieve an optimised level of security."

Amber's earnest desire to equip James with the skills to protect himself was palpable. While he was still struggling with the acceptance of these mindsets, he couldn't deny their logic. He was beginning to understand the value of resilience in cybersecurity, and although the road to acceptance was not easy, he took the first few tentative steps.

### *Over To You*

Review the second mindset: "Cybersecurity is not too complex, technical, or difficult for you." It's easy to be daunted by the jargon-filled, technical world of cybersecurity. But have you ever considered reviewing this mindset from a different perspective? Like the analogy of the locksmith, Amber used it to help James understand that being secured is a combination of choosing the appropriate tools in line with his online workflows, and habits, and you paired with cyber awareness, digital attitudes, and behaviour.

When you shift your focus to being secure, you will realise that identifying appropriate and relevant areas of cyber security to become secure should be less complex, technically manageable, and easy to learn.

### *Mindset #3*

*"Prevention is better than cure"*

Amber could sense the lingering doubt in James, but she gently pressed on. She knew the importance of the third mindset, 'Prevention is better than cure.' Drawing on the wisdom often imparted by parents to their children about health, she began to weave an analogy he could relate to.

"You know how your mother always told you to care for yourself so you wouldn't get sick? It's far less painful than going through the recovery process, right?" she asked. James nodded, recalling the countless times he'd heard those words. "The same principle applies here."

With the air filled with tension, she proceeded, "Yes, getting sick might help build immunity, but at that moment, you're just focusing on the discomfort and hoping to get better. Plus, there's always a risk that you might not recover. In the digital world, it's better not to 'get sick' - not to fall victim to a breach. Examples of this preventive measure include ensuring you have a reputable antivirus installed on your devices, using strong and unique passwords, using the VPN for secure connections, etc. Preventive measures to minimise your risk exposure."

Amber carefully pointed out, "But this doesn't mean avoidance. It's about taking necessary precautions within your control."

James found his thoughts straying back to his predicament as she spoke. He began to see the value in the advice he was receiving. What if he had taken some precautions? Could he have avoided the trap he had fallen into?

The realisation was slowly sinking in. His situation was distressing, and he found the recovery process tedious and daunting. His irritation flared momentarily, but he knew she was making sense. The logic of her words doused his frustration.

"I get it, Amber," he finally admitted, though still reluctantly, "A few preventive steps could have spared me this mess."

While his admission was a far cry from complete acceptance, it was a significant step towards understanding the critical importance of a proactive approach to cybersecurity.

Amber could see that he had not internalised this mindset yet, but he no longer rejected it outright. That was progress, she thought, and she would take it for now.

### *Over To You*

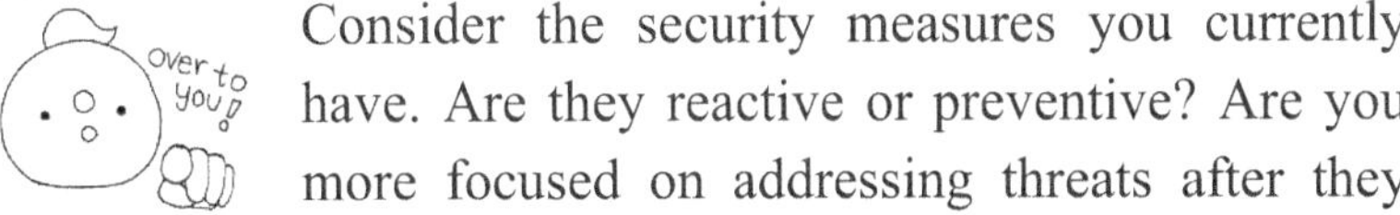


Consider the security measures you currently have. Are they reactive or preventive? Are you more focused on addressing threats after they occur, or do you strive to anticipate and block them? Do you also believe that prevention is better than cure (recovery)?

## *Mindset #4*

*"It is no longer a matter of if but when you will be compromised"*

Amber noticed James' confused expression when she transitioned to this mindset - "It's no longer a matter of if but when you will be compromised." It seemed contradictory to the proactive preventative mindset she'd just explained. However, Amber was ready for this query.

"James," she said, "I know this sounds like a contradiction. We aim to prevent cyber-attacks, but we also need to prepare for the eventuality of a breach. It's about resilience. And having an Individual Breach Recovery Plan is critical." Amber jotting her thoughts, said, "And we will discuss this plan in greater detail later in our discussion."

She lent on an adage for clarification, "We do our best and hope for the best, but we must also be prepared for the worst. It's like a fire drill at school."

Seeing James' eyebrows raise, Amber added, "Remember our primary school days, how our teachers always stressed fire prevention? At the same time, they conducted fire drills to prepare us for an unfortunate fire incident. It's the same with cybersecurity. We do our utmost to prevent, yet we stand prepared for a breach."

### *Over To You*

Consider the fourth mindset, "It's no longer a matter of if, but when you will be compromised." Initially, this can sound disconcerting, even contradictory. Have you ever contemplated the inevitability of a cyber breach? It may seem counterintuitive to prepare for an event you strive to prevent, yet this concept forms the bedrock of your resilience in cybersecurity. It's about taking every step to safeguard against cyber threats while being ready to respond effectively when a breach occurs. Think about this: Are you prepared for the "when" of a cyber-attack?

### *The Power of a Cybersecurity-Savvy Mindset*

Amber knew that if she could instil these mindsets within him, he would not only become more secure but could also inspire others to do the same. She envisioned him adopting cybersecurity practices as naturally as he would with personal hygiene habits. She hoped he would realise the importance of staying informed, being resilient, and prioritising security over convenience.

If James can internalise these perspectives, he is poised to improve his cybersecurity posture and create a safer digital landscape for himself and those he loves.

### *Over To You*

And you, the reader, journeying through this narrative, take a moment to reflect on these mindsets and their relevance in your life. Are you ready to step into the shoes of James and embark on your transformative journey? Does any of the mindset statement resonate during your reflection?

## *James' Digital Assets*

Thoroughly and systematically, Amber began delving into James' digital assets list. She dissected this personal assessment of five broad categories, namely:

- Personally identifiable information and sensitive data.
- Financial information.
- Login credentials and access.
- Digital assets and connected devices.

- Social connections and reputation.

She intended to dissect the allure of these assets from a cybercriminal's perspective, hoping to highlight why James was indeed a potential target of interest, despite his initial belief of insignificance. She elaborated on how a cybercriminal could abuse each asset as she went through the various categories.

James' eyebrows furrowed as he sought to understand why cybercriminals prized his Personal Identifiable Information. He expressed his confusion, seeking clarification from her, "I still can't get my head around why my data is so valuable to these criminals."

With a reassuring nod, Amber patiently expanded on her explanation, "Imagine your personal information as a key that can unlock various doors. With these keys, cybercriminals can gain unauthorised access to different parts of your life."

"Your Personal Identifiable Information," she continued, "like your name, identity number, and address, is unique to you. This information is not just a collection of random data; it is you in the digital world. When cybercriminals get their hands on it, they can impersonate you."

Amber explained the potential ramifications, "They can open bank accounts in your name or apply for credit cards. Imagine discovering one day that there are several loans in your name that you didn't apply for. That's one example of how your personal information can be misused."

"Moreover," she said, "having personal details like your address, phone number, or email address can make their phishing attempts more convincing. They can fabricate an urgent situation, such as a problem with your bank account, convincing you to click on a malicious link or provide further sensitive information."

Amber also touched upon the darker side of the digital underworld, "In the dark net, your data is a commodity. It can be sold to other criminals who may use it illegally. Your identity becomes their disguise, offering them additional protection while they conduct their operations."

"As disconcerting as it sounds," Amber finished, "your personal information is highly valued in the underbelly of the digital realm because it allows cybercriminals to exploit various aspects of your life without your knowledge. And that's why we must take necessary steps to protect it."

The stark reality of Amber's words sank into James. He now clearly understood that his personal data and digital identity were far from insignificant. It was a vital asset that needed robust protection.

Financial information, she explained, could be used to carry out unauthorised transactions, open new accounts, or commit fraudulent activities.

Then she moved on to Login Credentials, which, in the wrong hands, could grant unauthorised access to sensitive data or even result in identity theft or ransom attacks.

Amber touched on Digital Assets and Connected Devices, where cybercriminals could steal valuable data or control devices remotely for sinister purposes.

And lastly, she stressed the misuse of Social Connections and Reputation, underlining the risk of impersonation and fraudulent activities, damaging reputation, or spreading malware.

The vivid picture Amber painted of what cybercriminals could do with James' assets profoundly affected him. He could no longer deny the gravity of the situation. James was beginning to realise that these digital assets had significant value he needed to safeguard.

In her earnestness to drive the point home, Amber explained that a single cyber breach could ripple effect, initiating multiple subsequent attacks on James' contacts. She stressed that James needed to alert his circle about his breach, making them vigilant against messages in his name. She underlined that identity theft, ransom attacks, and phishing were just some possible threats that could emerge.

Amber emphasised to James that his cybersecurity measures were not just for his protection alone. He was also responsible for ensuring the security of his friends, family, loved ones and followers. His followers trust him, and in the unfortunate event of his account being compromised, it shouldn't be the cause of their online safety being jeopardised. She cautioned that cybercriminals could exploit such a breach to attack his followers.

Feeling the weight of her words, James was more willing to discuss how he managed his digital assets. With her tireless and detailed explanations, he was starting to appreciate the importance of his role in cybersecurity and the urgent need to adopt good cyber hygiene habits.

### James Managing his Assets

Amber had a series of questions[2] for James. She wanted to understand how James manages his assets. She started with a gentle tone, but her questions were pointed and relentless. "Let's talk about your digital assets. What types besides your Personal Identifiable Information, bank details, and login credentials do you own? I mean things like photos, videos, contract documents, passwords, and content."

---

[2] Go to Appendix 02. Identify, Manage, Organise and Monitor your Digital Assets.

James felt the weight of the questions and sighed, scratching his head as he attempted to answer. Amber's intensity didn't diminish as she moved on. "How do you organise and manage them? Do you use a specific folder structure or naming conventions? Do you tag or label anything?"

The questions kept coming. How do you secure your assets? How do you manage access to them? What about application access? James felt the pressure mounting as Amber meticulously dissected his cyber habits.

Amber continued, "What backup storage solution do you use? Local, external, cloud storage provider? Do you have a backup strategy? How often do you back up your assets, and where do you store the backups?" Her tone remained steady and factual, with a hint of empathy. She wasn't done yet. "Do you use software or tools to manage and store your assets? How do you manage digital files or backup software? How do you dispose of devices that store your digital assets?"

James, feeling the strain, paused to collect his thoughts. The questions were indeed gruelling, but he understood the purpose. His irritation slowly dissipated, replaced by a sense of appreciation for Amber's thoroughness. He knew it wasn't an interrogation but a necessary journey into the heart of his digital existence.

Fighting the urge to retreat, James met Amber's gaze and spoke calmly, "Alright, Amber, let's keep going. I understand this is for my good. After all, you're doing this because you care, right?"

Amber returned his gaze, her eyes softening with affection, "Of course, dear, I want the best for you. I want you to understand how crucial these measures are for your safety in the digital world." James nodded, the edge of his irritation replaced with determination and trust. The conversation continued; their bond strengthened in the face of this shared journey towards digital resilience.

## *James In His Digital Realm*

### *Heart-to-Heart Chat*

James had always been a frequent internet user, but it was more than just a tool for him; it was a window to the world, an extension of his life. His business thrived on it, his relationships flourished through it, and he sought solace during lonely times. Yet, as he sat across from Amber, he realised he hadn't quite comprehended the intricate web he'd been weaving.

In the quiet comfort of their shared space, Amber explained to James how his interaction with the internet was more than just a series of clicks and typed words. It was like leaving a digital footprint across the vast internet desert, a trail that could lead back to him if he wasn't careful.

"Every time you send an email, make a video call, post a status update, or even simply browse," She explained, her tone serious yet calming, "you're leaving traces of yourself. It's not inherently harmful, but it can be if it falls into the wrong hands. And that's where vigilance comes in."

James took in Amber's words, absorbing the gravity of what she was saying. He remembered the email about the resort, a potential outcome of his demand generation efforts, and realised the danger lurking behind each innocent-looking communication.

"But how am I supposed to identify these threats?" He asked, a flicker of worry crossing his eyes.

She smiled reassuringly, "It's all about knowing what to look for, James. Unusual emails, strange requests for personal information, suspicious hyperlinks - these are all warning signs."

Amber explained each potential threat, relating them to James' experiences to make them more tangible. She discussed the dangers of emails with grammatical errors, mismatched email addresses, and urgent calls to action.

What resonated with James the most was Amber's emphasis on unexpected contact and content. The mention of emails congratulating him on a project win he didn't remember bidding on made him sit up straight. Realising what could be hidden behind such an enticing lure was frightening.

"But I can't stop using the internet, Amber," He admitted, the trepidation evident in his voice.

"Of course not," She reassured, her hand gently resting on his, "and you shouldn't have to. It's about being smart, being vigilant, and knowing how to protect yourself."

In Amber's quest to protect James, she found herself drawn closer to him. And in his journey to understand the digital world, he discovered an admiration and respect for Amber's strength and wisdom.

Love and empathy served as their guiding lights in every struggle and challenge, illuminating their path and leading them towards a stronger bond. Their shared journey was a testament to the resilience of love in the face of adversity, a love story written amidst the complex tapestry of the digital age.

***Reasons for being on the Internet***

The cosy apartment Amber and James shared was an indication to their adventurous spirits, brimming with mementoes from their globetrotting escapades. Nestled in their shared living space, the two companions sat across from each other, an air of focused intensity surrounding them. Amber's sleek laptop lay between them, humming softly in the evening quietude, a modern-day Pandora's box poised to unlock the complexities of James's online life.

Amber's gaze was steady yet gently inviting. "James," she began, her voice reverberating with sincere determination, "Let's examine why you connect to the Internet. By understanding your reasons and your platforms of choice, we can devise a cybersecurity strategy tailor-made for you."

The conversation kicked off with James's communication as one of the reasons. "Emails, video calls, instant messaging… I use them all," he admitted, unconsciously reaching for his smartphone. His eyes sparkled with enthusiasm as he described his digital interactions with followers, collaborators, and friends. Yet, the seriousness of Amber's expression tempered his excitement. Aware of the unseen hazards lurking beneath the innocuous surface of these digital communications, she promised, "We will need to address secure communications." her fingers deftly typing notes on her laptop.

Next in line was the wide realm of research, a topic James approached with palpable exhilaration. He painted a vivid picture of the Internet's rich trove of ideas, his enthusiasm almost infectious. Though echoing his excitement, Amber warned him of the treacherous quicksand of false information and malicious sites. "Our focus will be on helping you discern reliable sources." she counselled, her eyes mirroring her serious intent.

The conversation shifted to James's collaboration efforts, his detailed account of using various online platforms for content creation holding Amber's rapt attention. His network of creative associates, storyboarding, video production, photo editing, audio recording, and scriptwriting - all pointed to a layered, complex online existence. Amber, the cybersecurity expert, noted, "Secure file sharing is going to be vital, James. We must protect your collaborative work," her mind already strategising the best defences.

James's engagement with social networking, a subject that visibly excited him, came next. His anecdotes about nurturing his online community elicited a soft smile from her. But beneath her empathetic understanding, her professional acumen warned of the potential risks of data leaks and online harassment. "Our strategy will include guarding your online identity. It's a treasure that needs careful protection."

Laughter filled the room as the topic transitioned to entertainment, with James sheepishly confessing his indulgence in online gaming and streaming videos. Amber, laughing along, warned him of the potential phishing scams disguised as game rewards or updates and ransomware attacks via game mod packs from unofficial sources.

As they ventured into Internet banking, Amber's surprise at James's infrequent checks on his transaction statement was concerning. "James, regularly reviewing your transaction statements, not just banking and credit card statements, but your online shopping statements, is a good habit. We'll need to add that to our strategy," she urged in a firm yet caring tone.

The mood took a light-hearted turn when they broached the subject of online shopping. With a twinkle in his eyes, James teased, "Well, Amber, you're no stranger to my online shopping habits. Remember those surprise packages that turn up at our doorstep?" Amber blushed at his words, a fond smile playing on her lips as she recalled the numerous tokens of his love.

Their earnest dialogue ended on a hopeful note. Amber, assured of her comprehensive understanding of his online life, was ready to craft a detailed cybersecurity strategy. On the other hand, he felt a surge of gratitude for Amber's meticulous efforts to protect his online identity.

### *Over To You*

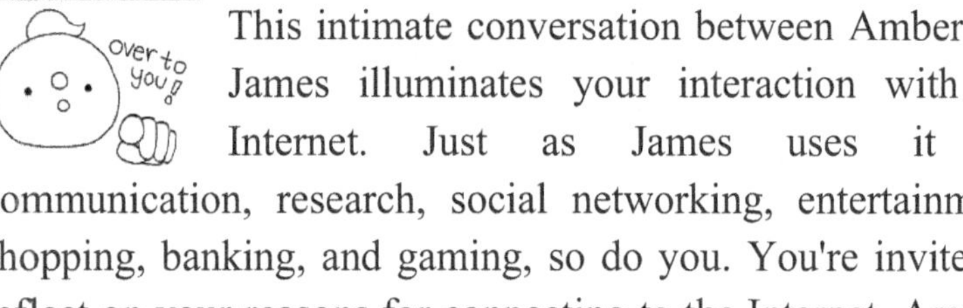


This intimate conversation between Amber and James illuminates your interaction with the Internet. Just as James uses it for communication, research, social networking, entertainment, shopping, banking, and gaming, so do you. You're invited to reflect on your reasons for connecting to the Internet. Are you aware of the risks involved with each aspect? Are you taking sufficient precautions to guard against cyber threats? As Amber reminds you, your online safety is your responsibility. It's time to take a closer look at your cybersecurity strategies.

### *How James Connects to the Internet*

The evening shadows had begun to retreat, revealing a living room bathed in the mellow glow of a single table lamp. The air was heavy with the lingering aroma of their shared dinner. Amber and James, comfortably nestled on their aged but cherished couch, were engrossed in an uncommon discourse that revolved around James's online posture. The room, a haven of shared memories, bore silent witness to their dialogue, the worn-out rug and the scratched coffee table reflecting their love, as old as the visible wear and tear around them.

"Alright, so James," She began, her tone loving yet firm, "walk me through your Internet routine again?" James, half-hidden behind his laptop screen, responded with an amused grin. He loved these moments - Amber playing 'tech guru' and him, the unwitting student.

"Well, I connect from either here or the café," he started, glancing up from his screen to meet Amber's gaze. Amber's eyes held a look of slight worry. The risk levels at each location were different and had their problems. She gently squeezed his knee in reassurance, a silent promise of guidance.

James's nonchalant narrative of his café routine elicited a grimace from Amber. The free Wi-Fi he so freely connected to was a hotbed of potential threats, a fact that she needed to impress upon him. She knew his Internet-connected wearables and Smart TV were potential portals for intruders. "I guess I need to be more careful, huh?" he said, noticing her reaction.

Amber was relieved when James spoke about his home setup. Their home Wi-Fi was a well-guarded fortress due to Amber's dedication and expertise. Secure behind a robust password and the latest WPA3[3] protocol, it was a safe harbour in the tumultuous sea of cyber threats. Amber listened with a furrowed brow as he dived into his data storage habits. His scattered approach to categorisation and blatant disregard for naming conventions were alarming. His assurance of having a method to his chaos did little to appease her. "It's like your sock drawer," she said, playfully nudging him, "You always know where to find the red-striped ones!"

Her playful banter ceased when Amber realised that James didn't have antivirus software, or a VPN installed on his PC, notebook, tablet, or smartphone. His blatant disregard for cybersecurity wasn't amusing; it was a glaring vulnerability.

---

[3] WPA3 is the latest and third generation of Wi-Fi-protected access, providing the most secure Wi-Fi security protocol through encryption and authentication available today.

Still, she didn't reprimand him. Instead, she reminded him gently, "Security isn't inconvenient; it's necessary."

As he spoke about his café habits, Amber couldn't help but frown. His obliviousness was a liability. It wasn't just about the free networks but also about his physical security. She could see he was unaware of the potential snoopers and CCTV cameras. His password was a hacker's dream. "Is my name part of your password?" Amber asked. James responded with a grin and said, "Of course!" "While that is very sweet of you, James, you should not have your girlfriend's name, our meeting anniversary, birthdays, or anything that makes it easier for the hackers to guess your password, as these are the first things, they will do in a brute force attempt to crack a password. We need to rethink your password." She suggested it, her voice veiling her deep concern.

James's open manner of holding virtual meetings at cafés was another red flag. Even though he was considerate enough not to disturb others, Amber knew he unknowingly shared his conversation with those nearby.

As she absorbed his digital lifestyle, her concern swelled. His lax approach to cybersecurity was evident, and he seemed blissfully unaware of the lurking dangers. His world was a cyber ocean filled with hidden threats. But as she looked at him, she felt a surge of determination. She was his lighthouse, and she would guide him safely through these turbulent waters. A playful flick of his nose brought an infectious smile to her face. This was them, Amber and James, a team ready to face the real and digital world. The atmosphere, although serious, was imbued with love, trust, and a dash of playfulness. As they sat there, the room hummed with the comforting silence of understanding and love, their bond stronger than any cyber threat.

### *James' Online Habits*

Amber continued with their discussion. She delved into James's online habits. She knew that habits could sometimes be a cybersecurity Achilles' heel. Yet, amidst the gravity of the conversation, they managed to maintain their playful banter, an occasional exchange of loving glances reminding them of the bond they shared.

Amber learnt that James, nestled in his plush armchair, would frequently use his tablet or mobile phone to surf the Internet, enjoying his movies and carrying out his research. However, creating and publishing his content had him turning to his desktop PC or notebook, their familiar hum a constant presence in their home.

His habits concerned her, especially when he mentioned that he often left his devices connected to public Wi-Fi in public places, even when idle. As he enthusiastically explained his routine, she couldn't help but frown.

"James," she began, her tone serious yet caring, "keeping your devices connected when you're not using them is like leaving the front door open when we're out. You wouldn't do that, would you?" He looked at her, surprise registering on his face, and shook his head.

She wanted to understand his safety measures when surfing. His admittance of occasionally bypassing Internet browser warnings and not knowing how to identify secured websites made Amber sigh, a moment of concern flitting across her face. Realising her concern, James held her hand, a silent promise to learn.

Her heart sank as she confirmed her suspicions about his casual approach to passwords and Wi-Fi security. Still, a sigh of relief escaped her when he mentioned automatic updates of his applications and operating system. His lack of caution about new applications, though, had her raising her eyebrows, a serious warning in her eyes.

Turning the discussion to data management, she inquired if James had backups and whether he regularly organised and cleaned up the data he collected. James' surprise at the question was evident, and he confessed that he had never thought about its connection to cybersecurity. She nodded, her eyes sparkling with affectionate reproach. "Cybersecurity is not just about tools, James. It's about habits too. Like keeping our data tidy."

When he said he didn't remove unused applications, Amber pointed out the potential risk, her hand tracing small circles on his arm in reassurance. She also urged him to consider his screen time, emphasising the need for breaks to remain alert.

During their discussion, Amber asked him about tracking his applications and subscriptions. As she talked, her words served as a reminder that familiarity was key to spotting abnormalities, a lesson James was coming to understand.

The evening wrapped up with a blend of laughter and learning. The seriousness of the topic was underscored by the playful yet intimate setting they shared, and by the end, James had begun to view his habits from a new perspective. It was a step closer to making his digital world safer and, for Amber, a step closer to peace of mind.

### Internet Breadcrumbs

As the evening wore on, the 'Zzz monster' spectre began to hover over James and Amber - an inside joke they've shared since they embarked on their romantic journey half a decade ago. But Amber was steadfast, resolved to delve deeper into the mysteries of Internet breadcrumbs before they yielded to the beckoning slumber. Their typical light-hearted exchanges had given way to a more sombre atmosphere as the conversation shifted to the nuanced world of cyber security.

"James," She started, with an earnestness that made him sit up straight, "Have you ever heard about digital breadcrumbs?"

James shook his head, his brow furrowing, "Sounds like something from a techy version of Hansel and Gretel."

She chuckled, a gentle reminder of their playful interactions. "In a way, you're right. But instead of a witch's house, these breadcrumbs can lead to a treasure trove of your personal information."

Amber described how these breadcrumbs, which are traces of one's online activities, could leave a comprehensive profile of a person's behaviour, preferences, routine, and interests. She explained the four categories: activity-based, identity-based, location-based, and device-based information.

"Your web browsing history, search queries, and even your online purchase history all come under activity-based information," She explained, holding up her fingers individually. "Think about it; whenever you click on a link or like a post, you leave a trace. All these add up and can be exploited."

James felt a shiver of unease. He considered his hours spent online, all those clicks and searches. He looked at Amber, his eyes filled with newfound concern. "And the other categories?"

Amber continued, explaining identity-based information like personally identifiable information and username/passwords, location-based information from IP addresses and location data from mobile devices, and device-based information like metadata and device specifics.

James was quiet for a moment, digesting all this information. "I've never thought about it that way," he admitted. "I mean, I knew the internet wasn't private, but I didn't realise I was leaving so much information just by being online."

She nodded, understanding his concern. "That's why we need to be aware, James. When we know what breadcrumbs, we leave behind, we can minimise them."

"But how do I do that, Amber?" He asked, looking genuinely worried now.

"Well, start using secure and private browsers[4], adjusting your social media settings, and being mindful of what you're clicking on. Using VPNs can help too. We can do much more, but these steps are a good start."

As Amber spoke, James found himself thinking about his online habits, realising how he had unknowingly left trails of digital breadcrumbs. It was a sobering realisation that left him committed to making changes. The cheerful atmosphere had faded into a more serious, contemplative one, filled with an understanding of the gravity of their online presence.

### *Over To You*

Their conversation that evening left a lasting impression on James and anyone listening. It is a powerful reminder that the digital world you traverse daily holds many unseen risks. But with awareness, caution, and a willingness to learn, one could navigate it safely, leaving fewer breadcrumbs for the wicked witches of the cyber world.

---

[4] Secure and private browsers are web browsers with features that protect your privacy and security while browsing the internet. Examples include Brave, Tor Browser, Firefox and DuckDuckGo.

The narrative journey that James and Amber have embarked on offers valuable learning moments that resonate beyond their living room's confines. Let's take a moment to reflect on these insights that could reshape your understanding of online presence.

Consider how James connects to the internet: at home or the café. Like many of you, he doesn't think twice about his digital habits, but do you ever consider the potential risks involved? Are you aware of the cyber threats lurking within unsecured networks in public spaces? Even at home, do you take necessary precautions, or do you, too, like James, remain oblivious?

Now, contemplate James' online habits. We leave our devices connected to Wi-Fi even when idle, not considering that this could open a door for cyber threats. How often do you disregard Internet browser warnings or neglect secured websites? James' relaxed attitude towards passwords, Wi-Fi security, and new applications mirrors your cyber hygiene. Are you guilty of the same laxity?

James' conversation with Amber highlights the importance of tidy data management and the need to keep track of your applications and subscriptions. Do you take the time to organise your digital assets and monitor your online subscriptions?

Finally, think about Internet breadcrumbs, a seemingly innocuous trail of online activity that can reveal a wealth of personal information. Do you realise how much data you're unintentionally sharing? Are you making conscious efforts to minimise your digital footprint?

Reflect on these questions and consider how your digital habits measure up. Are you, like James, carefree and uninformed, leaving a trail of breadcrumbs for potential cyber threats? Or do you take steps towards being more like Amber, aware, proactive, and protective of your cyber presence? You may want to take this opportunity to pause, reflect, and rethink your online security posture and habits. And consider what steps you can take to improve it.

As the morning sun winked through the half-drawn blinds, Amber turned to James, her eyes twinkling with curiosity. After a restful sleep, they were both rejuvenated, the promise of the long weekend creating a playful mood. It was the perfect time for Amber to probe into an area she had been pondering.

"James," She began, her voice light yet containing an underlying seriousness, "have you ever considered your digital risk appetite?"

James paused, his morning coffee halfway to his lips. His eyes met hers, intrigued. "Risk appetite? That sounds like one of your business terms."

Amber laughed, her contagious laughter filling the room. "Indeed, it's a term I often use in my consulting work, but I think it applies to our personal lives too, especially with digital security."

James set his coffee down, leaning back in his chair, his posture relaxed yet attentive. "Okay, Amber. I'm listening. What does my risk appetite have to do with cybersecurity?"

The room was filled with warm light, the sweet scent of morning coffee mixing with the faint aroma of the blooming flowers on their small balcony in the living room. Their kitchen table was a picture of a lazy morning: news of the day on their iPads, mugs of coffee sending up little spirals of steam, the remains of their breakfast adding to the homey feel.

With a cheeky competitive grin, Amber leaned forward to ask, "Do you remember the time we went go-karting?" James responded, "Yes, of course!" "You were very competitive on the track, but I still managed to win the race against you." He said it gleefully.

Amber responded, "Now think back to that go-karting experience. Your risk appetite determines how fast and daring you will go on the track. It depends on factors like your confidence, skill level, knowledge, experience, and how much thrill you're seeking."

James chuckled, picturing himself zipping around a go-kart circuit. "So, if I'm cautious and prefer to take it slow and steady, my risk appetite is low. But if I'm up for the adrenaline rush and take daring manoeuvres, my risk appetite is higher."

Amber nodded, her smile widening. "Exactly! Your risk appetite in go-karting influences your choices on speed, overtaking, and the level of risk you're willing to accept. Similarly, in the digital world, it guides your decisions on what activities to engage in and the security measures you should take."

She continued, tracing a finger along the rim of her coffee cup, mimicking the twists and turns of a go-kart track. "Understanding your risk tolerance is important because it helps you balance convenience and security. It determines how much effort and resources you will invest to protect your digital assets and maintain good cybersecurity. Much like go-kart racing, if your objective is to clinch the win, you must optimise speed while steering clear of any accidents. Therefore, you practise and learn the intricacies of the track to ascertain the best instances for acceleration, the safest strategies for surpassing opponents, and how to coordinate your body movements with the bends to maximise speed and momentum."

James nodded, the go-karting analogy making it easier for him to grasp. He glanced out the kitchen window, imagining the thrill of racing around a track. "I never thought about it this way before. It's a lot to absorb, but I see the importance now. I guess I've been too lax with my cybersecurity."

Amber's expression softened, a mix of pride and love in her eyes. "It's common to overlook these things, James. But being aware and having this conversation is a great step towards a more security-conscious mindset."

They sat in comfortable silence, with birds chirping outside, creating a serene backdrop. It was a new day, filled with possibilities, and they had the entire day to explore this topic further.

"You've given me a lot to think about," James admitted, breaking the silence. "And I realise it's time to start taking my cyber hygiene seriously."

Amber beamed with warmth and affection, knowing they were embarking on a journey towards better digital security. With each step they took together, they were building a stronger and safer digital future.

### *Over To You*

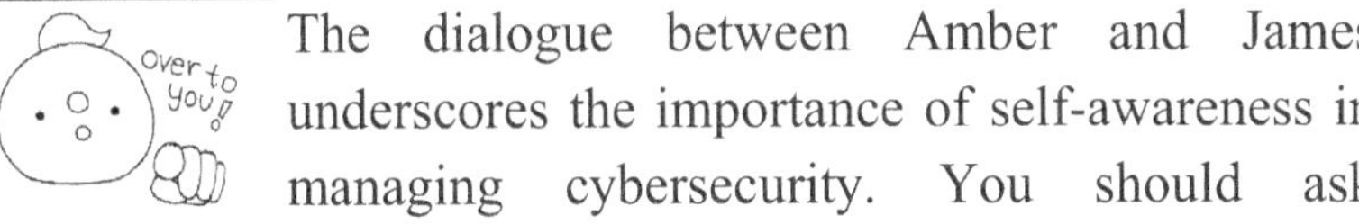


The dialogue between Amber and James underscores the importance of self-awareness in managing cybersecurity. You should ask yourself: Have you truly understood your digital risk appetite and how it influences your online behaviour and cybersecurity decisions? And your readiness to dedicate some time, money, and effort towards maintaining your online safety or 'cyber hygiene'? Consider using the go-kart analogy or any other analogy you can relate to involving risk to determine your digital risk appetite.

### *Amber's Findings*

Amber traced the remnants of their morning conversation with James in the soft glow of their shared living space. The cyber breach he had experienced was an awakening call, a jarring nudge directing him towards Amber for help to recover his accounts. She hopes the process will influence the adoption of good cyber hygiene habits. His compromised social media accounts, his windows to the world, were not just digital platforms; they were elements of his identity, his livelihood, and a passport to prospects.

Amber remembered the relief in his eyes when they discovered his Internet banking, online shopping, and online gaming accounts remained untouched. The passwords and two-factor authentication had served as a protective barrier. "Small mercies," she had whispered, her hand enveloping his in a silent promise of support.

Amber and James had spent the past day reaching out to James' contacts, encompassing friends, family, loved ones, corporate clients, associates, and a vast portion of his online followers. Their mission was to enlighten them about the breach of James' social media accounts, and they urged them to remain alert for any suspicious communication appearing to come from James, as this could be a cyber-attack. They continued asking for assistance to report on their behalf about James' compromised accounts to the respective social media platforms.

The sense of unity and togetherness had been overwhelming, much like the 'Aha' moments James experienced. He had been blissfully ignorant about his digital footprints, the breadcrumbs he left behind for the cybercriminals.

Amber found herself smiling, reminiscing about the surprise and enlightenment that filled James' eyes when he realised his assets' value and the vulnerabilities, he had been unaware of. The threats of not having an antivirus on his devices and his careless approach when working outside the home were all eye-opening revelations.

She had then taken a step further, shedding light on the workflow of connecting to the Internet, an ordinary act he had been doing for years. Yet, he had been oblivious to the sequence of activities that unfolded every time his devices connected to Wi-Fi or 5G.

Amber patiently explained, "First, we power up and connect our device, like a smartphone or laptop, to the Internet through Wi-Fi or a wired connection. Alternatively, we use cellular data, like 5G."

Once the connection was established, the digital world opened like a vast ocean before them. The browsing of information, communicating through emails or social media, indulging in entertainment through streaming services or online games, online shopping, banking activities, and remote work or online learning— all these activities seemed so ordinary yet were tied intricately to the digital world.[5]

The importance of secure logins was emphasised, especially with platforms requiring usernames and unique passwords. Amber stressed the importance of second-level identity verification (two-factor authentication) for added security.

She ended by reminding James about the importance of disconnecting the devices after the sessions, a step often overlooked in the hurry of daily life. The conversation that started with a playful tease had grown into a learning experience, a quest for awareness in the labyrinth of the digital world.

Thus, a typical day unfolded into an eye-opener for James, a newfound awareness that revealed the complexities and vulnerabilities of his everyday digital activities. It was a poignant reminder that each click, login, connection, and disconnect played a pivotal role in the grand scheme of cyber safety.

---

[5] Go to Appendix 03. Diagram: 3-Step Process to Connect to The Internet.

## *Know Thy Cybercriminals*

As the rays of morning sunlight continued to peek through the half-closed blinds, James and Amber refilled their cups with fresh coffee. In their relaxed kitchen corner, a playful aura swirled around the pair, intermingling with the seriousness of the topic at hand, cybersecurity.

With an amiable smile, Amber broke the silence. "James, knowing about cybercriminals, their motivations, targets, and techniques can be vital in protecting our digital lives."

James, comfortable in his casual morning attire, looked up from his steaming mug, his face reflecting intrigue and playful scepticism. "Ah, so it's a 'know thy enemy' thing, then?"

She chuckled, the pleasant sound resonating around their warm, homey kitchen. "In a way, yes. And in this case, it is about knowing what cybercriminals' motivations and activities are to everyday individuals like you and me," she replied. "Awareness. Detection and prevention are our first lines of defence. Knowing their tactics helps us recognise threats and avoid them."

As the birds chirped in the background, Amber outlined the profile of a cybercriminal. They could be an individual or part of a syndicate, leveraging digital tools for unauthorised access, theft of sensitive information, spreading malware, financial fraud, or even identity theft. James' eyes widened in response to each point. The casual, laid-back atmosphere suddenly held a touch more gravity.

"Their motivations can range from personal amusement, revenge, hacktivism, and financial gain," Amber continued. "Some just enjoy the thrill of breaking into secure systems, while others have political motives, pushing a certain agenda, or even for simple financial gain through scams and theft."

She pointed out that understanding cybercriminals' motivations helps predict what they might target. That understanding enables better personal security and more strategic risk management. This knowledge can aid in quicker response and recovery when a breach occurs.

He nodded, understanding dawning on his face. "So, if I know what they're after, I can better protect those assets."

"Exactly," Amber beamed. She then explained the types of assets cybercriminals often target. "They might go for assets with significant financial or strategic value, like customer databases, trade secrets, or sensitive information they can exploit. Assets that can be monetised quickly are also often in their crosshairs."

She emphasised how cybercriminals also look for easy targets-those with known vulnerabilities or weak security measures. High-profile targets are also attractive for these cyber criminals seeking fame in their community.

James looked thoughtful, his gaze shifting to their iPads lying on the table. "So, our devices can be seen as treasure chests to these cyber criminals, full of valuable, exploitable information?"

Amber nodded, her tone serious yet reassuring. "That's why we should consider cybersecurity a crucial part of our daily lives. Think of it as brushing our teeth or locking our doors-it should be routine."

James fell silent for a moment, absorbing her words. The birds continued to chirp outside their window, the world waking up to a new day. His gaze landed back on Amber, appreciation evident in his eyes.

"With everything we have discussed, you have convinced me that it's high time I started taking my cyber hygiene more seriously." He said.

A warm smile bloomed on Amber's face; her heart filled with pride and affection. It was a fresh start towards better digital security for both. And they were taking the first step together, armoured with knowledge and fortified by love.

In the end, the gravity of cybersecurity didn't dampen their playful interaction but gave it a new depth - a testament to their shared responsibility and care for each other. As the new day unfolded, they were more prepared, secure, and, most importantly, more aware.

### *Threats Targeting Individuals*

The Saturday late morning bathed Amber and James in a gentle cascade of sunshine as they moved and snuggled up in their living room. They embarked on a new conversation, the day's tranquillity starkly contrasting the digital storms they were about to traverse.

"Imagine," Amber began, her eyes sparkling with the thrill of exploration, "Your devices like a castle, home to all your precious jewels — data and information. But villains are lurking around, ready to raid."

The first threat was Phishing attacks. She explained, "These are like fake messengers trying to trick you into revealing your castle's secrets, maybe even inviting the villains inside."

Next, malicious attacks, like viruses, malware or ransomware and worms, were akin to hostile invaders launching a barrage on the castle, aiming to break in, cause damage or steal valuable treasures.

"Then, there's the Remote Access Trojan or RAT. It's like having an enemy spy in your castle, relaying every secret back to the villains," She continued, the image of a medieval traitor painting a vivid picture.

She then mentioned the 'Man-in-the-middle' attacks, "It's like a rogue courier intercepting your messages, stealing, or even altering them."

And finally, outdated systems and the 'Juice-Jacking' attack. "An old, crumbling castle is easy to breach, right?" Amber pointed out. "And using public USB ports is like inviting a stranger into your castle, who might be a villain in disguise."

Just as James was soaking in these cyber threats, Amber gently guided him to the next realm, the world of networking equipment. "Think of your router as the castle's gate," she said. "Now, imagine if you never changed the gate's lock from the one the builder installed. Easy for villains to break in, right? That's what happens with default password attacks."

"Firmware vulnerabilities are like weaknesses in the gate's design, just waiting to be exploited. And a Man-in-the-middle attack at this stage is akin to a villain impersonating a trusted visitor."

Amber then explained how weak Wi-Fi is like an open gate, inviting unwanted guests. And a 'Brute force attack' is like a persistent villain trying every trick in the book to pick the lock.

Amber steered James towards the browser and cloud platforms' world as they delved deeper into their Saturday morning exploration. She compared social engineering[6] to a master of disguise tricking the castle guard. The 'Watering hole[7]' and 'Lookalike domains[8]' attacks were like hidden traps on familiar paths, ready to capture the unwary traveller. "An unsecured website," she explained, "is like a risky,

---

[6] Go to Appendix 04. What is Social Engineering?

[7] It is a cyberattack that targets a specific group of users by infecting websites they commonly visit.

[8] Go to Appendix 05. What are lookalike domains, and how do we avoid them?

unprotected bridge you cross, where a villain can easily ambush you."

Finally, they ventured into the realm of the cloud platform. "Weak security settings are like leaving your castle doors open," Amber warned, "And a compromised Plug-in is like broken armour, exposing you to attack."

She spoke of malvertisements (malicious advertisements), comparing it to treacherous vendors selling poisoned goods and credential sniffing to a pickpocket stealing the castle's keys.

James listened, wide-eyed, the weight of Amber's words slowly sinking in. "So, every click, every login is like a step in a potential minefield. We need to tread carefully, always on guard," he mused, his first Eureka moment dawning on him.

Amber smiled, acknowledging his newfound insight, "And never forget, ransomware, scams, and phishing are the most common traps laid out by these villains globally."

James said, "I know scams and phishing, and I heard about this ransomware thing a lot in the news. But I do not understand what it is, how it attacks and whether it is relevant to individuals like us."

Amber responded, "Ransomware is malware that encrypts the victims' files and demands a ransom payment to decrypt them. It is like someone going into your room and stealing your diary. But instead of removing it, they make a copy of its content and lock it in a box and demand ransom to unlock it. They threaten to destroy or leak the contents of your diary if you do not pay the ransom. And James, it is relevant as it also targets individuals like us."

She added, "It is a very damaging and costly attack regarding the ransom payment and the loss of productivity."

James asked, "How is the ransomware virus delivered to us?"

Amber responded almost immediately, "In the same way as how all malware or viruses can be delivered to us, through phishing, social engineering, pirated software, free software, game modification packs, via drive-by downloads, malvertisements, Remote Desktop Protocol attacks, lookalike domains, watering holes and exploit kits. These are just some common ways it is delivered. And that is why we need to be vigilant."

James nodded, absorbing the information. "So, how can we protect ourselves against these ransomware attacks?"

Amber responded, "Great question! Here are some suggested measures to keep yourself safe from ransomware attacks. Firstly, using strong, unique passwords for all your accounts is essential. This enhances your account security and makes it harder for ransomware to gain access. Additionally, enabling two-factor or multi-factor authentication adds an extra layer of security. And do not share the verification codes generated during the authentication process with anyone."

Amber continued, "To protect your devices and network, update your operating system, software, and applications regularly. Installing reliable security software like antivirus or anti-malware can detect and remove threats. Enabling automatic updates ensures you have the latest security patches. Disabling macros and auto-run features provide additional protection. Consider using a VPN to encrypt your internet connection and avoid using public Wi-Fi for sensitive activities. Segmenting your network and limiting user privileges also help limit ransomware spread."

James nodded, realising the importance of data and privacy management. Amber explained, "Regularly backup your data to external hard drives or cloud storage and keep your backups up to date to minimise data loss. Be cautious of phishing emails, suspicious links, and attachments. Educate yourself about ransomware and be wary of social engineering attempts. Stay informed about the latest threats and cultivate a security-minded mindset with regular training."

Amber added, "If you notice anything suspicious, disconnect from the network immediately to prevent further ransomware spread. Having an Individual Breach Recovery Plan is also crucial to mitigate potential damage. Using browser and email filters can help weed out malicious websites and emails."

James looked at Amber, appreciating the depth of knowledge she shared. "Wow, there's so much to consider when protecting ourselves from ransomware. I didn't realise the extent of these risks."

Amber smiled and reassured James, "It may seem overwhelming, but by following these measures and staying vigilant, you can significantly reduce your risk of falling victim to ransomware attacks. In the case of ransomware, prevention is key. I will compile a ransomware checklist[9] to make it easy to remember."

As the story ended, James looked at Amber, his eyes reflecting a mix of worry and resolution. His second Eureka moment came as a deep understanding, "This cyber world is a bustling city that never sleeps with little enforceable laws like the great wild west of the past, and we are the warriors protecting our castle. We need to be ever vigilant."

### *Over To You*

Over to you!!

Having the appropriate security-oriented mindset and being digitally self-aware, helps us pinpoint vulnerabilities, strengths, and values in our online behaviours. Our devices resemble a fortress, a trove of treasures we must safeguard. Each threat, whether phishing,

---

[9] Go to Appendix 06. Protect Yourself against Ransomware Attacks.

a malicious attack, or lax security settings, is like a rogue lurking in the shadows. Let's remain alert, update our security systems, refrain from divulging sensitive data, and carefully guard the keys to our fortress. After all, your armour of awareness, security tools, good cyber hygiene habits, security-oriented mindsets, and more shields you in this digital arena.

Amber will delve deeper into safeguarding your digital world in the next chapter. She'll outline four critical pillars of defence: robust passwords, device and network security, data privacy, and online awareness. You will learn to view your digital presence like a kingdom to be secured, from guarding each digital entrance to keeping data locked safely away. By following Amber's advice, you'll gain the knowledge, tools, and habits to become digitally secure.

# CHAPTER THREE

## Protecting James' Digital Lifestyle

As the Saturday afternoon sun filtered through the living room, Amber and James nestled on their plush sofa, a cosy respite after a hearty lunch. Yawning lightly, James looked at Amber, his eyes heavy with the aftermath of their intense morning discussion. But Amber, driven by a fierce protective instinct, mustered the energy to press on.

"James," she began, her voice soft yet firm, "Your digital life is like a sprawling kingdom. To protect it, we need a master plan." She outlined four key pillars for his defence:

- Password – First Line of Defence
- Device and Network Security
- Data Security and Privacy Management
- Online Behaviour Awareness.

Amber began by outlining the overview of the four pillars: "The initial three pillars focus on fortifying your castle, while the fourth is about navigating safely outside of it, steering clear of traps set by cybercriminals."

She then introduces the first pillar, the first line of defence - passwords. "Imagine your password as the secret code to your kingdom's gate. It must be unique and strong like a riddle only you can solve."

She detailed the characteristics of a robust password - a mix of letters, numbers, symbols, and the avoidance of common phrases or personal information. The importance of uniqueness was underscored, "Each gate, or account, should have its unique code, so if one gate is breached, the others remain safe."

Amber introduced the concept of a password manager[10], akin to a trustworthy royal scribe who safely keeps all the secret codes.

Their conversation flowed into the realm of Device and Network security. Amber explained endpoint device security, likening devices to royal guards that must be well-equipped and alert. This means updating firmware, operating systems, and applications to remove potential vulnerabilities.

---

[10] A password manager is a software application that stores and manages your password. It generates unique passwords for all your online accounts, storing them in an encrypted database, giving you the security of your passwords. It is convenient because it can automatically fill in your login information on websites and applications. The other benefit is that it helps to minimise the risk of falling victim to lookalike domains and phishing websites. Your accounts cannot be easily compromised, giving you peace of mind.

Secure home networks, she explained, were akin to having a safe, fortified royal court. She emphasised the importance of setting strong network passwords, encryption, and updating the network's firmware.

On Data Security and Privacy Management, Amber warned against email and phishing scams, comparing them to treacherous spies aiming to trick the king into revealing his secrets. She highlighted the importance of data backup strategies, akin to having a secret, secure vault for the kingdom's treasures. "Being safe on social media is like being prudent at royal gatherings," she said, "Be careful of what you share and who you interact with."

Finally, Amber talked about Online Behaviour Awareness. She explained safe connections and browsing habits, "It's like choosing the right path to travel, avoiding risky routes, and ensuring your journey is secure."

She concluded, "I will go into great detail for these four pillars because our goal, my dear James, is to minimise your vulnerability. Like a castle with no weak spots, the more fortified we are, the more painful, time-consuming, and costly it will be for any invader to breach our defences."

As the afternoon waned, Amber and James leaned back, the weight of their discussion sinking in. Despite the day's mental strain, there was a comforting sense of preparedness. James looked at Amber, his gratitude mirrored in his weary eyes, "Our kingdom's safety is in good hands."

### *Over To You*

Protecting your digital kingdom requires a comprehensive plan consisting of strong and unique passwords, securing your devices and networks, managing your data security and privacy, and being aware of your online behaviour. Remember, you want to make it as difficult, painful, expensive, and time-consuming as possible for cybercriminals to breach your defences. It's your kingdom, and you must protect it.

## *Pillar 1*
### *Password-Protect Your First Line of Defence*

As the late Saturday afternoon sunbathed the room with a warm golden glow, Amber, energised by her mission, stirred her coffee, and prepared to delve into the realm of passwords. James, leaning forward, was ready to embark on this arduous journey to fortify his digital life.

"James," Amber started, her voice calm yet resolute, "A password is your first guard, shielding your digital kingdom, be it your devices, social media, online banking, shopping, gaming, and so much more. It's the sentry at the gates and has to be strong and unique." She paused, deciding to confront the demons before enlisting the angels. "But first, let's talk about the bad and vulnerable passwords."

She spoke of common weaknesses in passwords - the obvious suspects like '123456' and 'qwerty', the shorter ones with less than eight characters, and the ones that spelt out personal information like birth dates or names. She elaborated on the dangers of using default credentials and shared passwords. "These, my dear," she said, "are like weak guards susceptible to the enemy's tricks. And if you use the same password across all your accounts, it's like having the same key for every room in the kingdom - one breach, and everything falls."

James nodded affirmatively and remarked, "I can relate to experiencing my entire social media empire crumble."

As they munched on some snacks, Amber presented James with a password checklist[11], her personal 'Strength-o-Meter' for passwords. James, upon evaluating his passwords against the checklist, grimaced. His passwords were weak and reused across multiple accounts. But Amber reassured him, "The good news is, you can start afresh. With strong, invincible guards."

Then she shared her guidelines for creating these strong sentinels. "Imagine a password like a knight's armour. The stronger and more intricate it is, the more invincible the knight." She recommended passwords of 12 to 14 characters, including various character types, and avoiding personal information and common words. "No two knights should wear the same armour. So, no two accounts should have the same password."

Amber introduced James to a password manager, a digital 'squire' capable of creating, managing, and storing all these unique, strong passwords. "With this squire at your side, you only need to remember one strong master password. It will handle the rest for you."

She detailed the convenience, accessibility, and additional security layers password managers offer, such as two-factor authentication and monitoring against breaches. "James," she concluded, "this squire could be the handiest ally in our digital kingdom." But she didn't stop there. She introduced James to a website that can determine the password's strength and how long it will take to crack it.

---

[11] Go to Appendix 07. Password Checklist.

She cautioned against using actual passwords for these tests but to use one with a similar pattern. They used the 12-character password 'Apprehensive' example, identified 'Astonishment' as an equivalent, and tested the password's strength 'Apprehensive'. The test results startled James as he reviewed the results below.

As they observed the time it would take to crack various versions of a 12 characters password, starting from 'astonishment' consisting of only lowercase - taking three weeks to break, to progressively stronger variations:

- 'astonishment' – all lowercase – 3 weeks
- 'Astonishment' – 1 uppercase and lowercase - 300 years
- 'AstonIshMEnt' – 4 uppercase and lowercase - 300 years
- 'Ast0n1shMEnt' – 3 uppercase, lowercase and 2 numbers - 2,000 years
- '@St0n1shMEnt' – 3 uppercase, lowercase, 2 numbers, and 1 special character - 34,000 years
- '@St0n1shME&t' – 3 uppercase, lowercase, 2 numbers and 2 special characters - 34,000 years

James was amazed by the significant increase in password strength and the level of protection it could offer when a password consists of mixed character sets of uppercase, lowercase, special characters, and numbers.

Amber, wanting to add to James' amazement, introduced passphrases and said, "Have you ever considered using a passphrase instead of a traditional password? It's usually longer and made up of whole words or sentences. For example, 'I enjoy hockey' or simply 'Ienjoyhockey' can make remembering important security codes easier."

James, waking from his astonishment, asked, "A passphrase? I've never heard of that before. What makes it different from a regular password?"

Amber continued, "Well, instead of a jumble of letters, numbers, and symbols in a password, a passphrase is a sentence and can be longer than a password as it includes regular words. It is like a password in a sentence. It is usually relatable and, therefore, easier to remember. It can be more secure if chosen wisely. It also becomes harder to crack when you use mixed characters of uppercase, lowercase, numeric and special characters."

James, placing his hand on his chin, said, "That sounds impressive. That would be easier to remember without compromising on safety."

Amber said, "Exactly! It's a great way to keep things like your computer or online accounts safe. Would you like to try creating one together to see how long it takes to crack one?"

James responded curiously, "Sure, let's give it a try. How about 'I love pizza'?"

Amber replied, "That's a perfect example of a 12-character passphrase. Well done! You see, it's simple yet effective."

James: "Wow, another new learning today."

As they experimented, James could not believe how easy it was to create simple, easy-to-remember, strong, and unique security codes. Applying the passphrase 'i love pizza' to the same test setup as they did with the password, he quickly noticed the substantial increase in the time required to crack the passphrase.

- 'i love pizza' – all lowercase – 54 years
- 'I love pizza' – 1 uppercase and lowercase - 12,000 years
- 'I Love PizzA' – 4 uppercase and lowercase - 12,000 years
- 'I L0ve P1zza' – 3 uppercase, lowercase and 2 numbers - 63,000 years
- 'I L0ve P1zz@' – 3 uppercase, lowercase, 2 numbers, and 1 special character - 400,000 years
- 'I L0ve P1$z@' – 3 uppercase, lowercase, 2 numbers and 2 special characters - 400,000 years

James excitedly commented, "I wished I knew about this earlier! I will start using passphrase as my new password for my login credentials. I cannot believe how easy it is to create and remember them. Plus! They are more secure."

Amber continued and highlighted the importance of regularly changing passwords. Amber explained, "James, even though it may take a significant amount of time to crack a strong password, it is still crucial to change your password regularly, ideally every 3 to 6 months. This practice helps enhance overall cybersecurity and reduces the risk of potential breaches."

James nodded, realising the significance of this practice. By changing passwords regularly, we can protect our personal information and stay one step ahead of cybercriminals, right?

Amber smiled, glad that James understood. "Exactly! But what would be better is to be informed when a specific platform that our account with a specific user ID is on, has been compromised. Taking immediate action to change the password of that account will reduce the risk of that account being breached. And we will discuss this next."

The conversation left James feeling more empowered and committed to maintaining good password hygiene, knowing it is crucial to protecting their online security.

## Over To You

The significant importance of having strong and unique passwords becomes evident from the discussion between Amber and James. The importance of a password manager, two-factor authentication, and the power of robust passwords stand highlighted. So, you should armour your digital kingdom, making each guard unique and strong. In the realm of cybersecurity, your vigilance is your strength.

## Passwords and User-ID (Two Peas in a Pod)

Under the soft lighting of their late afternoon setting, Amber decided it was time to wind down their intensive digital defence discussion, paving the way for their much-needed dinner and drinks outing. She regarded James, her eyes reflecting the satisfaction of one productive day dissecting cybersecurity's intricacies. "James," she began, "I know it's been a marathon. How are you holding up?"

James shrugged, his initial irritation giving way to appreciation. He had started this journey with one sole aim: to recover his breached account. Now, he saw a bigger picture unfold. Amber wasn't just fixing his problem; she was equipping him with the knowledge to prevent future ones. She was helping him build a strong foundation for a secure digital life, making cybersecurity accessible and understandable. He nodded, "I get it now, Amber. I see why it's important to be cybersecurity-savvy."

Amber then guided James through the importance of user IDs, a concept as crucial as passwords but often overlooked. She explained that user IDs, much like passwords, needed to be used wisely. "Think of them as different gates in your digital kingdom, James. Each gate leads to a different section of your kingdom, and should a breach occur, the damage is contained within that section."

She recommended having five user IDs as a layered defence strategy.

- For personal work and side hustles.
- For personal, official stuff, including financial activities.
- For social media.
- For paid online accounts and e-commerce.
- For fun/burner accounts.

She explained that this segmentation strategy creates clear boundaries within his digital environment.

Amber also stressed the importance of monitoring these accounts for suspicious activities and any signs of unauthorised access.

She introduced James to a website; a database designed to track and notify when a user ID has been compromised.

https://haveibeenpwned.com/

"James, always keep in mind that constant vigilance is essential. Performing routine checks every three months and taking swift action can aid in safeguarding your digital realm. Furthermore, this tool has a particular feature that can alert you if there's a compromise. As I stated before, obtaining this information lets you promptly change your passwords for those affected accounts, thus reducing the possibility of a full-scale account compromise."

As they prepared to head out, a shared understanding of expectations and perceptions about cybersecurity echoed between Amber and James. James now understood the significance of a holistic approach to cybersecurity, moving beyond his initial focus on recovering his account. His eyes held a newfound respect for Amber's work and the complexity of the cyber world.

### *Over To You*

Passwords and user IDs are important in the realm of cybersecurity. Remember, each element of your digital defence – your passwords, user IDs, and vigilance – forms an interdependent, fortified barrier against potential breaches. Your security is as strong as you make it in this digital era. So, let's take a leaf out of Amber and James's book and begin your journey toward a safer digital life.

## *Pillar 2*
## *Device and Network Security*

On a bright Sunday morning, Amber and James sat at the dining table in the kitchen, sipping hot cocoa. They had spent the past one and a half days discussing James's online habits and how to keep him safe in the digital world. They start their day discussing how to secure James' devices and network equipment connected to the internet.

First, Amber asked James to list all his gadgets that could access the internet. "Well, there's my desktop computer, notebook, tablet, and smartphone," James began. "And I can't forget my gaming console, smart TV, and watch!"

Amber nodded, jotting down everything. She explained that all these things were like doors into James's digital castle or house. The more doors he had, the more he had to ensure they were monitored and locked so that no intruders could sneak in. The first way to do this, she said, was to make sure each device had a strong and unique password, just like a good, sturdy lock.

Amber also talked about outdated operating systems and firmware. She compared these to rusty, old locks that burglars could easily pick. "And don't 'jailbreak' your smartphone or iPad," she warned. "It's like leaving your backdoor wide open for anyone to walk in."

She cautioned James about applications he didn't use anymore, explaining that these were like windows that had yet to be opened in the last six months. They might not seem important, but if neglected, they could provide an easy entry for a sneaky intruder. "If you don't use them, it's better to uninstall them," she advised.

Amber also advised James to exercise caution when downloading free applications from unverified sources. She further elaborated, "Although most apps are harmless, some can be used to infiltrate your devices for harmful purposes. It's always better to play it safe."

Amber also warned about misconfigured equipment. It was like having a door with a lock not installed correctly. "A poorly installed lock is almost as bad as no lock at all," she said.

When they moved onto the subject of Internet of Things (IoT) devices, Amber highlighted their vulnerabilities. She explained that using weak or default passwords on these devices was like hiding a house key under the doormat. It was the first place a thief would look.

She reminded James that sometimes, the real danger was not from a mysterious internet hacker but someone who could physically steal his devices. "That's why we must keep our digital 'valuables' safe," she emphasised.

Lastly, Amber warned about the dangers of rogue Wi-Fi networks, comparing them to cunning thieves disguised as friendly neighbours. "Your devices might connect to these, thinking they're safe, but it's just a trick," she said.

James felt a new responsibility as the morning sun warmed the kitchen and living room. Amber's words had shown him the many doors and windows he had in his digital castle or house and the importance of keeping them all secure. But he also knew that with Amber's guidance, he could do it.

### *Over To You*

Like James, I am sure you have several devices connected to the internet, each a possible entrance for a cyber burglar. Amber's advice reminds you that you must care for every device like you would your home. So, ask yourself: How secure is your digital home or castle?

### *Protect PC and Notebooks*

Amber and James decided that changing their environment would be refreshing. Amber asked James, "Shall we head to the nearby Café to continue our conversation over coffee?"

James nodded, thinking that it was an excellent idea. It was a quaint café around the corner from their condo. Once they arrived, they ordered two cups of coffee and a slice of cheesecake to share. Settling into the plush, comfortable armchair beside the huge window. Amber began their conversation on cyber hygiene as they indulged in the cheesecake. They'd already spent a day and a half diving into James' cyber habits, and Amber was about to unveil the next chapter in their journey.

"So, James," Amber began, an earnest glint in her eyes, "securing your personal computers and laptops is essential. You don't want to leave any windows open for cybercriminals, do you?"

James shook his head, leaning back into the armchair. "No way, Amber. I've got my whole life on these devices. I'll be lost without them."

Amber responded with a soft smile, appreciating James' openness and commitment. "The first step is to ensure that your apps and operating systems are always up to date. Updates often contain fixes for security weak points found in older versions. But these updates don't just improve security; they also bring in new features and functions for the product."

While James scribbled notes, Amber continued, "Maintain only the apps you actively use. Unused apps can serve as potential backdoors for cyber threats. They're just an open invitation for hackers if they aren't supported anymore."

 James looked up, frowning. "And what about my phone?"

"Ah, good question," Amber said. "Reviewing and deleting apps that don't run on the new operating system is crucial on your phone. It's like clearing out the clutter in your house, ensuring everything runs smoothly."

James nodded, processing Amber's advice. She picked up her coffee, taking a sip before launching into the topic of antivirus software. She emphasised the importance of using a reputable provider and installing the software on all of James' devices.

For Amber, creating both an administrator and a user account was paramount. "By having separate accounts with unique passwords, you limit system-wide changes and encourage secure habits. Think of it as having a fortress wall around your most precious items."

They dove deeper into secure browsing, discussed two-factor authentication, secure Wi-Fi practises, and using a Virtual Private Network (VPN) for added protection. Amber, glowing with passion for her work, explained, "Two-factor authentication is like having a second lock on your door. It's an extra step. Yes! But it adds another layer of protection. The key to the second lock is like your one-time password (OTP). If a hacker somehow gets your account password, they won't be able to access your account without the OTP, often a code sent to your phone. And remember, do not share your OTP with anyone."

James responded with understanding, "I see, so it's similar to having a sturdy lock on your front door but also having a secured iron gate in front of it, and each lock requires a different key."

"Exactly," Amber confirmed, "And remember, safe Wi-Fi practises are also key. Public Wi-Fi networks are usually not secure, which makes it easy for someone else to intercept your information. If you can, use your mobile data instead when you're out and about."

James interjected, "But what if I have to use Wi-Fi outside?"

Amber smiled and said, "That's where VPN comes in. A Virtual Private Network, or VPN, creates a secure tunnel for your data. It's like your data is on a secret road, hidden from everyone else."

Amber then ventured into physical security measures, underlining the importance of biometrics, and securing devices against unauthorised access.

Amber also warned James about the potential dangers of connecting USB devices to your computer, such as external hard drives or flash drives, especially if you need clarification on their origins or safety. "There's something else we need to discuss," she began. "USB devices - things like external hard drives or flash drives." James nodded, indicating his familiarity with these devices. "Yeah, I use them quite often for transferring files and backups," he said.

Amber frowned slightly, looking directly at James. "Well, it's important to be careful with these, especially if you're not entirely sure where they've come from or if they're safe. They can carry hidden dangers," she explained.

"Dangers?" James echoed, his voice carrying a hint of surprise. "How is that possible? When I brainstorm new ideas with my team, we often share them on thumb drives to refine the content." James seemed visibly stressed, "Are you suggesting that I can't trust my team?"

Amber chose her words carefully as she responded to the complicated situation. "It's not exactly about trust," she began, "but about potential risks. Malware or viruses can infect trusted or untrusted devices, jeopardising all your data. This is one common way these threats spread." Recognising she hadn't highlighted this point enough, she continued, "You must take steps to guard yourself, and one important measure is to install a reputable antivirus software on your devices." She added, "It will inspect thumb drives before you access their content. This extra step will help you identify and eliminate potential threats before they infect your computer."

James queried, his voice filled with worry, "What about my team?" Amber responded, "Well, if they were like you before we started this chat, I'd be quite worried about their cyber posture." Then, she gave James a playful grin, saying, "But maybe, once we finish our discussion and you start taking steps towards cyber security, you could share this knowledge with them!"

"Remember," Amber said, standing to stretch, "security and control should be prioritised over convenience."

As they paused to sip their coffee, looking out the large window on this perfectly warm and sunny Sunday, James fell silent, lost in thought. The weekend had been a voyage into the labyrinthine world of cybersecurity, and he felt better equipped to navigate it.

As Amber collected her notes, she watched James in his reflective moment. His brow furrowed in concentration; he was the image of a man resolved to make a change. Amber couldn't help but feel a sense of accomplishment. James has begun internalising the knowledge and tools to protect his digital life.

### *Over To You*

Amber and James' enlightening dialogue serves as a critical reminder to you about the importance of cyber hygiene in today's interconnected world. Reflecting on the exchange, you're encouraged to step back and evaluate your digital habits. Are you prioritising convenience over security? Are you mindful of your applications or devices connected to your computers? The story isn't just about James securing his cyber world; it's a thought-provoking call to action for you all to be more vigilant and proactive in protecting your digital life.

### *Smartphone and Tablets*

A gentle wind murmured through the foliage, creating a symphony of rustling leaves. The day was serene and picture perfect.

Amber continued the conversation, "As we covered before, securing your computer is paramount. However, I want to stress that it's equally vital for you to secure your smartphones and tablets."

James, showing a hint of confusion, turned to Amber. "I appreciate that smartphones are indispensable. They offer convenience, connectivity, various modes of communication, and many other applications and features." he confessed, "But to me, they seem quite invulnerable. The few cyberattack reports I've stumbled upon primarily focus on large companies. I've hardly heard of personal cyberattacks, especially those via mobile phones." James queried, scepticism lining his voice, "Is it crucial to amp up the security of our handheld devices? What havoc can a breach on a typical person's mobile really wreak?"

Amber responded with a soft chuckle, shaking her head slightly. "Your phone, James, is as powerful and vulnerable as your laptop or computer, if not more vulnerable. It's like a smaller, more mobile version of your PC. And just like your computer, it needs to be secured."

 James took a sip of his coffee, his eyes reflecting his intrigue. Amber began detailing the steps of securing mobile devices.

"The first measure you could take is to turn off your Wi-Fi when it is not required," Amber began. "This action wards off the possibility of your phone latching onto insecure networks, or what we call 'evil twin networks'."

James, taken aback, asked in disbelief, "Evil twin network? Are you joking?"

Keeping her composure, Amber patiently explained, "No, James, this is quite serious. An evil twin network is a fraudulent Wi-Fi access point set up by a malicious entity. This setup disguises itself as a legitimate network using the same or similar network name (SSID), often found in public places like coffee shops, malls, airports, or café like this one. Because of their very similar names, it's possible to mistakenly connect to a malicious network without realising it. Next, suppose the malicious network is using the same name as a legitimate one you have connected to before. Your device may automatically connect to it without your knowledge, potentially putting your device at risk. This allows the bad actor to intercept your network traffic, steal sensitive information, or initiate further attacks."

As James absorbed this information, Amber added, "That is why turning off the auto-connect feature on your devices is essential. It will protect you from inadvertently linking to these hazardous networks." She emphasised, "And let's not forget physical security; it is important to safeguard your devices against theft, just as you would safeguard your wallet or keys."

"That makes sense," James acknowledged. "What about updates, though?"

Amber gave a nod of approval at his question. "It's best to do updates on a trusted Wi-Fi network. Also, enable remote wipe and tracking features. If your device gets stolen, you can erase your data and track its location."

As they delved deeper into mobile security, Amber emphasised installing applications only from trusted sources like Google Play or the Apple Store.

"Exercise caution when apps request access to your information and resources," she cautioned. "Examine the credibility of the app and the developer and review their data privacy policy. Ask yourself whether the permissions they seek are truly required." Amber chuckled, "But honestly, it is understandable that most people don't read the terms and conditions or data privacy policy, but I would suggest doing a quick Google search about the app to see if there are any adverse reports associated with it."

James rubbed his chin thoughtfully, "I recently read that QR codes can pose a threat."

"You're right," Amber affirmed. "You need to exercise caution when scanning QR codes or clicking on shortcut URLs. They might offer convenience but can redirect you to malicious websites."

Amber elaborated, "I am often wary of them as they do not provide visibility into the destination URL, making it challenging to discern if they are harmful. That's why it's crucial to have antivirus software installed on your mobile device. Most reputable antivirus vendors offer mobile versions."

James admitted, "That's news to me."

Amber added, "In my view, having antivirus and VPN on your mobile device is even more critical than your PC because of the potential and possibility for cyber mishaps waiting to occur. We'll review this topic in greater detail when we discuss fostering healthy online habits and behaviour."

Transitioning to another cyber safety measure, Amber advised, "It's wise to allocate specific times to review and respond to emails and messages. If you're in a rush, you might overlook phishing or deceptive message attempts."

She then drew from her professional experience, "I've witnessed multiple instances where a hurried executive quickly scans a message, missing tell-tale signs and inadvertently clicking on a link or downloading a malicious file."

She elaborated, "Worse still, the smaller display area on a mobile device makes it even harder to identify the visual hints of a malicious message or email - hints that are easier to spot on a larger screen. I highly recommend allocating dedicated time for reviewing messages and emails when relaxed and not under pressure."

Drawing a deep breath, Amber concluded, "Finally, it's important to revisit and adjust your privacy settings on your operating system, apps, especially social media apps, cloud apps, and others, to ensure that they are configured to safeguard your data."

James leaned back, his thoughts swirling with the influx of new knowledge. He inhaled deeply; his gaze fixed on the leaves fluttering beyond the café window. He began to understand that his laid-back approach to his phone and tablet had exposed his devices, and himself, to potential threats.

The realisation hit him hard. He'd taken for granted the power and potential risks he held in his pocket. Amber's patient explanations echoed in his mind, reinforcing the importance of good cyber habits.

### *Over To You*

In this captivating conversation between Amber and James, you're reminded of the silent yet omnipresent threat of cyber vulnerabilities. Like many of you, James undervalued securing his mobile devices, viewing them as immune to the threats looming over large corporations. Amber unravels the unsettling reality - your indispensable smartphones are just as, if not more, susceptible to cyber threats as any computer. Through their dialogue, readers are enlightened on steps to fortify their mobile devices against cyberattacks - from disabling Wi-Fi and auto-connect to scrutinising application permissions, being cautious with QR codes and URLs, and diligently adjusting privacy settings. The story urges you to shed your casual approach towards mobile cybersecurity, encouraging you to consider the potency of the potential dangers you carry in your pockets daily.

The couple briefly paused their discussion and decided to indulge in a shepherd's pie and a sultana pastry. Amber mentioned, "Just like we nourish our minds, it's equally important to nourish our stomachs." James grinned, his mouth full of the delightful sultana pastry, savouring its sweet taste. As they finished the last bits of shepherd's pie and pastry, Amber started discussing the next topic: securing the home network.

Amber started the conversation, her voice steady and confident, "James, since I set up our home network, I am not worried about it, but for your learning pleasure," she said with a broad cheeky grin, "I'd like to guide you through what I've done for you to be aware of the security measures we've got in place."

A soft smile playing on his lips, James leaned in, placing a gentle kiss on Amber's lips. "I can't thank you enough for ensuring our home network's security," he said, his voice filled with genuine gratitude.

Amber smiled and explained her comprehensive measures to fortify their home Wi-Fi network. "A robust, distinctive password safeguards our network," she detailed. "We use state-of-the-art encryption - WPA3, ensuring our communication remains private and protected."

She added, "Avoid using WPS or Wi-Fi Protected Setup because it is susceptible to brute-force attacks."

She continued, "By deactivating remote management access, which means turning off the ability to access our home network router from a distance, outside our home, I've warded off potential intrusions from external sources into our router configurations. And with network encryption activated, our data security is further bolstered."

She asked James, "Have you ever questioned or realised why I give you a new password each time your friends come over?" Taken aback, James confessed, "Honestly, I did not notice that." Clarifying her strategy, Amber revealed, "We have an exclusive network account just for guests, and with every guest visit, I reset the password. This way, we control their access to our network."

Captivated by her foresight, James complimented, "You're ahead of the curve! So, in a way, you've established a 'guest lounge' within our Wi-Fi network?"

Amber chuckled, "That's a creative interpretation, but yes. This strategy ensures our data is beyond the reach of our guests." She reiterated a point from their previous discussions, "Remember, it's not about not trusting your friends but about reducing our exposure to potential risks."

She added, "I activated our router's built-in firewall[12]. Our firewall's firmware is always up to date, providing optimal security, and the plug-and-play feature is disabled, adding an extra layer of protection. To top it all, I've segmented the network."

As James processed this, Amber clarified the implemented steps, underlining their importance. "Firstly, I changed the default credentials of our router's administration access. I used a strong, unique password, incorporating upper and lowercase letters, numbers, and special characters."

---

[12] A firewall is a network security system that monitors and controls incoming and outgoing network traffic based on predetermined security rules.

Amber steered the conversation back to the fundamental concept she had shared with him before. "Remember, dear," she said, "As we had discussed earlier, passwords serve as our initial barricade. They help manage access to devices, applications, databases, and internet connections."

James nodded, absorbing her words. Amber continued, "And don't forget, to further enhance the protection, we couple passwords with two-factor authentication wherever possible. It's like adding an extra lock to our digital doors. The default network name or SSID has been changed to something unique, personal to us without using any personal information."

James, absorbing all this information, nodded his head, "Is that all? "

Amber added, "I've also implemented MAC[13] address filtering. It lets us define which devices can connect to our network based on their unique MAC addresses. Lastly, our network is 'invisible' due to the disabled SSID broadcast. This doesn't make us invincible but adds an extra security layer."

James said, "Everything you have described makes a home network sounds like a fortress. I am appreciative and comforted with everything you have done to secure our home."

As the conversation winded down, James was quiet, reflecting on Amber's effort and her belief about the importance of cybersecurity. Amber's words echoed in his head, a reminder of the silent battles fought daily to keep their digital lives safe.

---

[13] A MAC (Media Access Control) address is like a unique identifier or "name tag" that every piece of hardware with a connection, like a computer, smartphone, or router, has. It ensures that data sent over a network reaches the correct device.

It was a war with invisible enemies with invisible weapons, fought not on battlefields but in the quiet comfort of homes, offices, and cosy living room corners. And in that war, Amber was his steadfast guardian, defending their data and digital lifestyle. It suddenly dawned on him that he had been the weakest link in Amber's cyber defence strategy.

### *Over To You*

As Amber meticulously narrates her well-rounded strategies, you are guided through the invisible labyrinth of digital defence, illuminating the necessity of safeguarding one's virtual boundaries.

It also highlights the profound truth that your ignorance can become a threat in this digital warfare. This narrative offers a reflective moment for you, prompting you to question your cybersecurity practices. Like James, are you the weakest link in your home network's security? It provokes you to realise that the guardians of your digital world are not just professionals and security solutions; they must act as sentinels, turning your homes into cyber fortresses, but you, too, must do your part.

You must all strive to be an 'Amber', ceaselessly fighting the invisible war, fortifying your cyber frontiers, and eliminating vulnerabilities, minimising the weakest link's risk exposure.

### *Securing Online Gaming*

Engrossed in their digital defence session, Amber grinned at James, "I think you've been good and deserve a nice lunch, don't you?" She chuckled, "Once we're through with this pillar, I'm sure you'll appreciate our meal more, not just for the taste."

"Next, we need to cover something you do not indulge in often, and that is online gaming," Amber shifted her tone, maintaining the seriousness of their discussion.

Amber began, "Even though you aren't a frequent gamer, you do indulge occasionally, and that's enough for it to be a potential risk."

Amber glanced at him and said, "James, just like you wouldn't neglect the security on your notebooks or smartphones, online gaming demands the same vigilance. Be it on gaming consoles or PCs, the principles remain the same."

She straightened up, her hands emphasising, "Primarily, never underestimate the importance of regular updates. This applies to every aspect, the console's operating system, each game, and all software you employ."

Her eyes held James's, ensuring he grasped the gravity of her words. "Understand this, James; each update is a guardian in its own right. They often come packed with patches, new game scenarios and features; simultaneously, it fixes known vulnerabilities, shutting the door firmly in the face of potential cyber threats."

James scribbled notes as Amber moved on to the second point, "Remember our password talk? It applies here as well. For your gaming accounts, ensure you use a strong, unique password, don't recycle passwords from other accounts, and activate two-factor authentication (2FA) to strengthen account security."

She described phishing attempts, warning James to be wary of emails, messages, or friend requests from unfamiliar sources especially the ones asking for personal information or login details.

Amber highlighted the significance of privacy, advising James to be cautious with sharing personal details on gaming platforms. "These details can include your real name, location, age, or sensitive information. You want to enjoy and win your game and not lose your identity," she quipped.

Amber leaned in; her expression serious. "Please understand the risks associated with downloads. Always choose games from trusted sources and avoid mod packs that aren't verified." She gestured as if sweeping away a lurking danger. "Cybercriminals are clever, and they sometimes embed malware in Mod packs. Their goal is simple: to infect your computer, hijack your account, steal sensitive data, or even install ransomware to extort money."

She paused, letting the implications settle. "You use a single desktop computer for various activities - online gaming, video and audio production, photo editing. Why is that?" she asked, her gaze steady on James.

James, momentarily taken aback, offered a simple explanation. "Well, this machine is a powerhouse. It has a high-end graphics card, a lot of RAM memory, a powerful processor, and a large hard drive. It suits all my requirements perfectly."

Amber nodded, her mind weighing the risks. "What if, one day, this computer is compromised through online gaming? What happens to all your work?"

James blinked, a new worry dawning on him. Amber continued, "Here's a suggestion. How about maintaining separate desktop computers? One dedicated to gaming and the other for your professional work. This could act as a protective measure if there's ever a cyberattack through your gaming activities."

Concluding her point, Amber imparted a word of caution, "James, you must grasp the gravity of this situation. There's a worrying shift happening. Cybercriminals are progressively setting their sights on gamers. We cannot leave any room for risk."

Amber looked at James with a playful grin and said, "I suppose you already know what I'll be getting for your next birthday gift, which is just around the corner." She winked at James, adding a touch of mystery.

Regaining her poise, Amber continued, "Your gaming console and PC should be connected to a secure network, preferably the 'guest ' network we've already set up. This minimises the chance of our primary network falling into jeopardy."

Amber paused, summarising their conversation, "We've covered a lot today, haven't we? But all this isn't just about securing your accounts, James. It's about fostering a secure digital lifestyle. Not just for you, but also for our friends, family, and eventually, maybe our children."

James nodded, visibly taking in all of Amber's advice. "Thank you, Amber. I've never thought of all this. It's a lot to process, but I see how vital it is. It's not just about a single password or one account; it's our entire digital existence."

### *Over To You*

Amber's meticulous walkthrough of securing one's online gaming experience highlights an often overlooked yet vital aspect of cybersecurity. Brimming with practical advice, this conversation reminds us that every digital activity, even casual gaming, comes with potential risks.

The narrative urges us to consider their digital interactions' depth and breadth, sparking a reflective moment. It highlights the importance of continuous learning in an ever-evolving digital landscape, where each interaction leaves digital footprints that could lead cybercriminals to our doorstep.

James' awakening to this reality is a mirror for us, inviting us to review our digital practices. It is a call to action to become our own 'Amber' to be proactive, knowledgeable, and secure in our digital playground. After all, we are the central characters in the grand scheme of our digital lives.

### *Securing IOT and Wearables*

Amber leaned back in her armchair, giving James a serious yet compassionate look, "James, when we talk about securing our digital lifestyle, we're not only talking about ourselves. It's for our friends, our families..." Her voice trailed off, replaced with a mischievous grin, "And maybe even for our future kids."

James chuckled, the weight of the situation dissipating slightly in the light-hearted moment. He nodded, indicating he was following Amber's line of thought.

With the stage set, Amber dove deeper into the concept. "The nature of cyber threats is like a chain reaction. Cybercriminals will aim at our network, friends, and family if we get compromised. Your recent breach is a testament to this," she indicated towards James's laptop.

Seeing the concern on his face, she reassured him, "Remember, we warned as many people as possible in your network about your breach so that they're alert against phishing attempts in your name. If each of us applies this vigilance, we're building a human firewall, one person at a time, securing not just ourselves but our whole community."

James was silent momentarily before finally replying, "Makes sense, Amber." His acknowledgement was met with a satisfied nod from Amber.

"Excellent! Now, let's move onto the last topic in this pillar before we break for lunch," Amber announced, adding with a teasing smile, "I hope you've thought about what you want to eat."

Shifting her attention to the digital display before them, Amber began discussing the Internet of Things (IoT) and its potential security threats. She explained that James's Smart TV and other connected devices must be on the secure guest network to limit access and potential breaches.

"Consider your fitness tracker," she said, glancing at the device on his wrist. "Health data privacy is a growing concern. I don't mean to repeat, but password discussion cuts across many security areas." She paused to breathe and said, "Use unique passwords, enable two-factor authentication, update regularly, and limit data sharing. Remember, James, security is not a one-time event but an ongoing process."

The advice flowed freely from Amber, touching upon the use of secure Wi-Fi networks, the necessity of updating firmware, the value of turning off unused features, and the importance of monitoring network activity. She encouraged James to adopt two-factor authentication whenever possible, physically secure his devices, and even segment the home network to enhance protection.

James replied to Amber confidently, "I know my network is secure, given that you're the one who set it up. Thank you so much!!!"

As Amber concluded her explanation, there was a contemplative silence. She shared much information, but the underlying message was clear: In the digital age, security isn't a luxury but a necessity. The reflective moment was heavy but empowering.

James broke the silence with a resolute tone, "Let's secure my digital life, Amber." She smiled, satisfied with his response. In reply, she assured him, "Indeed, we will, James, together. There are still a few more aspects we need to address."

### *Over To You*

This narrative is an important reminder of the interconnectedness of our digital lives and the shared responsibility we have to one another to ensure our security. It paints a compelling picture of the cascading effects of a single cyber breach, the impact on immediate victims, and potentially reaching friends, family, and even our broader networks.

Amber's wisdom underscores that your digital security habits do not just protect you individually; they contribute to a collective 'human firewall'. The story leaves you reflecting on your digital security practises and prompts a question: are you doing enough to secure your digital life and those people within your network?

## *Pillar 3*
## *Data Security and Privacy Management*

In a quiet corner of a renowned Omakase restaurant, Amber and James savoured a delightful Japanese lunch. The meticulous attention to detail, from the exquisite food to the charming ambience, left them enraptured. Yet for James, it wasn't the culinary artistry or the soothing atmosphere that heightened the experience; it was the woman seated across from him.

"Amber," he confessed, raising his eyes from the sushi platter, "it's moments like these, creating memories with you, that are truly priceless." He took out his phone, capturing their joyous moment in a selfie, and then, looking deep into her eyes, gently kissed her. Amber responded warmly, feeling a sense of contentment swell within her.

Following their enjoyable meal, they returned home, the afternoon sun casting long shadows. Amber felt the drowsy pull of a post-lunch nap, but much was still to be done. She headed to the kitchen to brew a pot of strong coffee to continue their conversation, as improving James' cyber hygiene was far from over.

"James!" She expressed, "I'm eager to wrap up our conversation quickly so we can start implementing real measures to boost your security." To his surprise, James echoed her sentiments, "You're right; I find myself genuinely intrigued to learn more." Amber was taken aback by James' response, anticipating some form of pushback from him.

Their conversation moved to the third pillar of cyber security. Data security and privacy management.

Amber warned James about the topic's complexities, assuring him she had endeavoured to create a clear, understandable structure. There will be overlaps and repeats of some of the topics discussed earlier. Amber reassured James that once you understand the fundamentals of cyber hygiene, cybersecurity, and the different techniques to improve the security posture, you will find that those foundational approaches are applicable when protecting other areas of your digital life.

As they waited for the coffee to brew in the living room, James held Amber's hand, expressing his appreciation. "I'm starting to grasp all of this, thanks to you," he said, his words genuine.

"You're quite the smart cookie. I'm fortunate you're my girlfriend and perhaps, one day, something more." The promise in his words filled Amber with warmth.

With a fresh cup of coffee warming their hands, they sank into the sofa, Amber once again taking the lead.

Amber introduced the topic - data security and data privacy Management. And highlighted to James that there are several things to cover in this pillar from the perspective of an individual.

- Assess current privacy and security status.
- Strong and unique password with two-factor authentication.
- Update software and device regularly.
- Be cautious with personal information.
- Review and manage application permission.
- Use encryption and secured connections.
- Regular backup and backup strategies.
- Educate yourself on phishing and scams.

- Regularly review and delete unnecessary data and applications.
- Create an Individual Breach Recovery Plan.

As Amber's words filled the room, James listened intently, realising the enormity of the digital world's risks and the essential role of privacy management. They spent the afternoon sipping coffee and talking about cyber security from not just an educational viewpoint. Still, it was a stark reminder of their shared responsibility to secure their digital lives. As the afternoon sunlight slowly edged into the living room through the balcony, their shared journey into Data Security and Privacy Management was only beginning.

### *Current Privacy, Security Settings, Strong and Unique Passwords & Two-Factor Authentication*

Amber savoured her coffee, comfortably seated with James in their living room. James broke the calmness, commenting, "Cyber security does not seem fairly complex." Amber acknowledges, "Yes, it's not, and I hope you are getting it." Amber added, "It is time to assess the current privacy and security settings on your social media and online apps. To make sure that they are as tight as they can be."

James expressed, "I'm yet to regain access to my social media profiles. Could we focus on my creative and cooperative tools instead? I'm referring to the software I use for video, audio, and image editing, which I utilise in collaboration with my fellow creative team members."

Amber responded, "We've taken all the necessary steps to recover your account. It's now with the social media platforms to review, investigate, and get back to us. We will politely follow up with them if we still await a response within a few days. Let's now move on to the other apps at hand. And the first thing we need to do is review the strength of your passwords on each online app." She then turned to James and asked, "Are you using the same password for all the apps?" Raising one of her eyebrows. James sheepishly responded, "I have not had a chance to change them yet because I just learned about strong and unique passwords yesterday."

Amber said, "There is no time like the present, go get your notebook, and we will change them together right now. At the same time, we will install a password manager and walk you through how to use it. We might as well install antivirus software as well as VPN."

She also told James that she would set up two-factor authentication on those online applications that have them. He smiled broadly and said, "Thank you so much for helping me."

Amber felt a sense of achievement after changing the passwords on James' online applications, setting up two-factor authentication, and installing antivirus software and VPN on his notebook. James felt that his notebook is now secured. Amber also changed the privacy management settings of his online applications.

She told James, "We will do the same for your social media accounts when we have recovered them."

This entire process took them longer than they had expected. By the time they completed the setup, it was time for dinner. Amber said to James, "Let's take a break. Let's go out to have a nice dinner later." She added, "We can continue discussing data privacy and the rest of the items after dinner. James nodded in agreement.

***Software and Device Update and Be cautious with personal information.***

Nestled in a diner nearby, Amber and James savoured a satisfying dinner of burgers and fries, their appetites still somewhat satiated from their exquisite Japanese Omakase lunch. They continued their enlightening conversation about the cyber hygiene and security concepts they had been examining over the past two days. Amber detected a spark of curiosity and anticipation in James' eyes as he enthusiastically recounted his insights into online safety and cyber habits.

"I had no idea that a larger portion of cyber security revolves around strategies and methods with only a smaller portion on the security technology," James confessed. Amber, wearing a knowing smile, replied, "I'm glad you caught onto that. Most people assume it's heavily tech-based because of the abundance of information and publicity focused on cybersecurity solutions."

She continued, "Unfortunately, most materials and solutions target corporate entities. I feel cybersecurity materials for individuals are not comprehensive, leaving individuals to make sense of these bits and pieces of information to their situation."

Suddenly, a thought struck Amber, "James, when you say that you've got it, or rather, you're beginning to grasp it, are you just saying so because I am your girlfriend?" James responded earnestly, "Not at all. You know me. Until this late morning, I found cybersecurity to be a burden, an inconvenience, always requiring extra steps for ordinary tasks. Your explanations and the reasons behind each step have given me a clear understanding of its importance and value. This understanding has helped me appreciate not just cybersecurity but also you. You've made a difference."

James gently took Amber's hand and continued, "Your explanations were straightforward, and the steps you guided me through were manageable."

Intrigued, Amber queried, "Do you think it would be worthwhile to translate what we've been working on into a book so that others could benefit from it?"

James replied, "Absolutely! You are incredibly intelligent and an excellent facilitator. Sharing your knowledge and experience would greatly benefit others. The challenge lies in persuading them to purchase the book or enrol in the course." Amber grinned back, teasing, "Well, that's where I have you!" her grin broadening at the playful remark.

James and Amber resumed their dinner, ready to return to the apartment to continue their conversation.

It was already 8 pm when they got back to the apartment. The air outside the balcony was still. They could hear some insects beyond the balcony.

Amber went to the kitchen to prepare warm chocolate for them to drink to continue the discussion. Amber is still wondering whether they will finish this pillar tonight, but she knows James is increasingly more open to learning about cybersecurity and cyber hygiene.

Both settled into their sofa in the living room. Amber opened her laptop and reached to take a sip of her hot chocolate.

She began, "We've previously discussed software and device updates. Do you have any lingering questions in that area?"

Brimming with confidence, James assured her, "I feel quite comfortable with it, but I'd like to use this opportunity to recall what you've taught me."

Amber responded with an approving smile. James said, "Essentially, it's about ensuring all the apps and the operating system on my laptop, desktop, tablet, and smartphone are updated whenever I get a notification." He elaborated, "Some devices might require firmware updates, which I will perform when notified."

With a sense of triumph, James stood tall. He explained the rationale to her, "The reason for staying updated is not just to benefit from the latest features and functionalities of the software but also to rectify any vulnerabilities that might have been detected unbeknownst to us." Overwhelmed with pride, Amber rose and enveloped James in a warm, heartfelt embrace, feeling truly proud of her man.

Amber proudly continued with the following topic: being cautious with personal information. Amber turned to James and asked, "You share much on your social media platforms. Do you think it's possible to maintain your authenticity, a trait that's attracted your substantial follower base while refraining from disclosing personal details?"

James was taken aback by the question, uncertain of how to proceed. "Oh dear, I'm not quite sure how to approach this," he confessed. Amber gently suggested, "James, to maintain your authenticity, you could continue sharing your thoughts, impressions, viewpoints, and perspectives regarding your travels. Make sure to shed light on your personal experiences and perspectives."

She added, "I'm certain your followers would be eager to hear your take on the quality of accommodation, the staff's friendliness and efficiency, the overall atmosphere, the location's convenience in public transport and amenities, and whether it's good value for money. They'd be interested in hearing about the unique experiences the location offers, your food and dining experiences, and any practical tips and recommendations you have for enhancing their visit. Does that sound reasonable?"

James mulled over the question and confidently asserted his agreement.

He inquired, "In our previous discussions, you mentioned the risks of oversharing. Could you explain what you mean by that?"

Amber clarified, "Consider the potential implications to your or someone else's privacy when considering what to share. If it infringes on others' privacy, it's better not to share it. Similarly, if it could compromise yours or others' personal safety, you should refrain from posting it. And if you're uncertain about the content, it's safer to withhold it."

"To help you consistently make the right decisions, would you like to work together to create a content guide[14] that outlines what and how you'll discuss your topics? It might seem strange initially, but it will become a natural part of your process with practice. Does that make sense, James?" Amber inquired.

---

[14] Go to Appendix 08. A Guide to Creating Authentic and Appropriate Cyber-Safe Content.

She further warned James that not every website is designed to handle data securely, and he should ensure the URL starts with HTTPS.

James was deep in thought, considering Amber's advice about withholding sharing if it risks privacy or raises doubts. He requested that Amber provide an example that could compromise his privacy. Amber suggested, "For instance, avoid announcing your vacations on social media while you are on vacation." James interjected, "But travel and vacation sharing is what I do!" Amber calmly responded, "I wasn't finished. You can still share about your vacations and resort stays, but do it once you're back home. You wouldn't want a potential cybercriminal tipping off a burglar that your house is vacant or that I am alone at home."

James nodded, understanding the logic behind Amber's advice.

She then stressed the importance of regularly checking and adjusting the privacy settings on his social media platforms and applications.

Amber stressed, "Always review your content carefully before you publish. Once it's out there, even deleting it won't completely erase it from the internet."

Amber concluded, "By being mindful of these aspects, you would be able to better protect your privacy and security."

### *Review and Manage Application permissions.*

Amber asked James, "Do you want to continue, or are you tired and would like to call it a night?" James responded, "I am still good and pumped from a previous topic.

Let us continue and see how much more we can cover."

Amber responded, "Okay, let us keep going, but please let me know when you are too tired and would like to tap out. We can always continue tomorrow since it is a national holiday. Anyway, another important aspect we need to discuss is application permissions. You know, the 'Allow Access to' messages you see when you install or run an app?"

James nodded, sipping warm chocolate, "Yeah, I've seen those. I usually just hit 'Allow' to get the app running quickly."

Amber's eyebrows raised as she cautioned, "James, you must exercise caution. Whenever an app requests access to sensitive resources like your device's camera, microphone, or specific data folder. It would be best to evaluate whether access to those resources is crucial for the app's core functionality. Mindlessly granting permission without considering the purpose and relevance of the request can compromise our privacy and security."

James scratched his head, "You mean the app could misuse these permissions?"

Amber shared a concerning example: "One of my friends had an app on her phone that had access to her microphone. The app could potentially listen to her conversations without her knowledge or consent. And another app with access to her photos, could view and upload those photos without her explicit consent each time. It reminds us how certain apps can invade our privacy and misuse the permissions we grant them."

"That's creepy!" James exclaimed, clearly taken aback.

Amber nodded, "It certainly can be. And it's not just about personal data on your device. Some apps collect usage data, tracking your activity within the app or even your location. This data could be used for marketing, but in the wrong hands, it could also be used maliciously."

"So, what can we do about it?" James asked, looking concerned.

Amber suggested, "The key is being aware and in control. When an app asks for permissions, please take a moment to consider why it needs them. Is it necessary for the functionality of the app? If it's a photo editing app, it makes sense to access your photos, but why would it need that if it's a game?"

"Make it a habit to review the permissions of your installed apps regularly and revoke any unnecessary ones. Most apps have settings where you can see and control these permissions."

James nodded, understanding the significance, "Got it. I'll be more cautious about the permissions I grant and review the ones I've given already."

"Good!" Amber replied, "Being mindful of these things can significantly enhance digital safety."

### *Use Encryption and Secure Connections.*

Late into the night, a fervour of enthusiasm energised James and Amber's lively discussion. As they dived further into their conversation on data security and privacy management, Amber cast a thoughtful glance towards James. "Shall we shift our focus onto two important aspects, Encryption and secure connections? How much do you know about them?" she queried.

Continuing their conversation on data security and privacy Management, Amber looked at James thoughtfully, "Now, let's talk about Encryption and secure connections. Are you familiar with these terms?"

James looked thoughtful for a moment, "Somewhat. I know Encryption has something to do with converting data into code so others can't understand it, right? As for secure connections, I think it means the data being transferred between two devices is protected?"

Amber smiled, pleased, "You're on the right track. Encryption is about converting data into a form that can't be understood by anyone who doesn't have the right key to decrypt it. And a secure connection usually refers to an encrypted connection."

She continued, "When sending or receiving data, if it's not encrypted, anyone who intercepts it can read it. It's like sending a postcard. Anyone who gets their hands on it can read your message. But if it's encrypted, it's like sending a letter in a locked box where only the person with the right key can open it."

James frowned, "That sounds risky. Why wouldn't all data be encrypted, then?"

Amber explained, "There can be complexities in implementing Encryption, and some systems may not support it. But as individuals, we can make choices that prioritise Encryption. For example, when using Wi-Fi, it's safer to use a secured network that requires a password because it's likely to be encrypted."

Interrupting Amber, James queried, "Didn't you mention something about WPA3 while we were discussing network security?" Amber's face broke into a pleased grin as she replied, "Ah, someone has been paying attention!"

She continued, "Exactly, WPA3 is the newest protocol for Wi-Fi Protected Access, ensuring our conversations are encrypted and safeguarded, preventing unauthorised access or eavesdropping."

"However, it's a different story with public Wi-Fi networks. We can't be certain about their security protocols, even if they require a password for access. This means that there's still a risk of your data being visible to anyone within the vicinity." added Amber.

James looked concerned, "I've used public Wi-Fi a lot in the past, especially during my travels."

Amber nodded understandingly, "Many of us do. But moving forward, using a Virtual Private Network or VPN is better when you're on public Wi-Fi. A VPN creates a secure, encrypted connection even over an unsecured network."

Amber paused and thoughtfully asked, "Do you think having a cyber hygiene cheat sheet[15] with do's and don'ts for travelling would be helpful?" James enthusiastically responded, "Absolutely! It would be a great reminder, especially since I frequently travel to review and share my experiences of new resorts and nearby amenities. I could also include tips for staying cyber safe while travelling." Amber's smile widened as she exclaimed, "That sounds fantastic!"

---

[15] Go to Appendix 09. Be Cyber-Safe on Overseas Holidays and Business Trips.

Amber picked up where she left off, "And when browsing the web, look for 'HTTPS' in the website address. That 's' stands for 'secure' and means the data you send to that site is encrypted."

James expressed understanding, "Alright, I remember you bringing up HTTPS when we were discussing safeguarding personal information. So, is this something I should always keep in mind?"

Amber responded, "In a perfect world, we'd always use encrypted and secure connections. In practice, it can depend on what you're doing. If you're browsing news sites, Encryption is less crucial. But Encryption is essential if you do anything involving personal or sensitive data like banking, shopping, or sending emails. Consider it your first line of defence for your data privacy management."

"Got it," James said enthusiastically, "I'll be more cautious about using Encryption and secure connections from now on."

"It's getting quite late. We should probably wrap this up for today. I know you're worn out, and I want you to know I appreciate your effort to simplify this for me and make it a smooth learning experience. You've earned a good night's rest." James expressed his gratitude, his eyes filled with affection for Amber.

Agreeing with him, she gave a tired nod, and they both started preparing to retire for the night.


### *Regularly Back-up your Data*

As the new day dawned, Amber and James were found in the kitchen, absorbed in the morning ritual of preparing breakfast and brewing their coffee. Once they settled comfortably at the kitchen table, James looked at Amber from his coffee cup, "Shall we dive into the next topic."

Amber looked up in surprise, her eyes twinkling. She flashed him a delighted grin, "Absolutely. Let's get into it!"

Picking up her coffee, Amber took a thoughtful sip, "So, today, we're going to discuss the importance of regular data backups. Do you know about the 3-2-1 backup strategy?"

James tilted his head, shaking it in amusement. "The numbers game again, huh? Enlighten me, please."

"Alright, smarty pants," Amber chuckled. "The 3-2-1 strategy stands for three copies of data on two different mediums, one kept offsite. In the event of data loss, you have multiple options for recovery. Pretty straightforward, right?"

James frowned slightly, thinking, "Could you give me an example? That might make it clearer."

Amber nodded, her face lighting up as she presented a relatable example. "Sure! Let's say; for instance, you have a digital photo album of our last vacation on your laptop. That's the first copy of your data.

For the second copy, you might want to invest in an external hard drive or SSD[16]. So, you back up your photo album onto that external drive. That's two copies on two different mediums, both local."

---

[16] Solid-state drive (SSD) is a storage device that utilises flash memory for data storage. Unlike traditional hard disk drives (HDDs), which have moving parts, SSDs are faster, providing quick data access, making them ideal for gaming, video editing, and reducing boot times. SSD storage is becoming popular due to its speed, durability, and lower power consumption than HDD storage.

Pausing to make sure, James was keeping up, she continued, "For the third copy, which needs to be offsite, you could use a cloud storage service. You upload your photo album there. In this way, if anything happens to your laptop or home, you still have a backup of those precious memories. That's the 3-2-1 backup strategy in a nutshell."

James sat back, looking thoughtful. "I see. So, I have three copies of my data spread across different locations and devices. That certainly does seem like a smart way to safeguard my data."

Amber grinned, pleased. "Exactly, smarty pants! You've got it. It's all about reducing the risk of loss."

James nodded thoughtfully, "Yes, that makes sense. Is there anything I need to do to prepare my data for backup?"

Amber carefully responded, "Actually, there is, and I am hesitant to bring this up. But since you asked, I would like to suggest improving the way you manage your data. You need to set up a good naming convention that makes it easy to carry out data housekeeping activities."

James looked interested, "Naming conventions? You mean naming a document 'project 01-Bali' is not a good idea?"

Amber laughed, saying, "No, but it could be better. James, what happens when you have 15 projects on resorts in Bali? How would you find them easily? Here is what I am suggesting. Naming files should be descriptive and potentially follow a format that includes information like the date, subject, and version. Using your document example, I suggest the name be [date]-[project category]-[version]-Bali-[name of resort]. For example, 2021-07-25-vlog-01-Bali-Resort James.

This makes searching easier and helps prevent accidentally deleting something important." "That's a good idea," James commented.

James enquired. "You brought up cloud storage earlier, didn't you?"

Amber grinned, "Ah, the magic of the cloud! As per my early example, cloud storage can be a useful part of your 3-2-1 strategy - it's an offsite storage solution. But remember, just like with your physical data, you need to organise your cloud storage and ensure its security. Good practises include categorising your files, regularly cleaning out unnecessary data, and using two-factor authentication and Encryption whenever possible."

James, rubbing his chin, mused, "Looks like I have a lot of data housekeeping to do."

Amber laughed brightly, "You're already a data management pro. Ready for another cup of coffee to boost your upcoming cleaning spree, champ?"

Their morning was filled with laughter and playful banter; both refreshed and ready to tackle the day's tasks. The kitchen echoed with their shared amusement, the warm sunlight spilling through the window enhancing the cheerful atmosphere.

### *Learn to Recognise Phishing & Scams*

As James and Amber made themselves comfortable on the living room sofa, Amber glanced at James, her face serious but gentle, "It's time we tackle phishing and scams, James."

James sighed, his mind returning to the recent incident that rattled him. "That's about what happened to me recently, right?" He asked, already knowing the answer.

"Yes, James," Amber affirmed, her voice a blend of sympathy and sternness as she gently held his hand. "Your case is a perfect example to start with. You remember the email from the so-called company that wanted to sponsor your trip to Japan?" James nodded, a pained expression crossing his face.

Amber continued, "That was a classic phishing scam. The email was crafted meticulously to look like a genuine sponsorship offer. The appealing content, the urgency to click the link and fill out a form, and even a supposed briefing document to download. It was all a ruse to get you to expose your personal information."

 James frowned, feeling the embarrassment and regret all over again. "I see that now. I was so eager about the opportunity that I didn't even think twice about it," he confessed.

"That's what they count on, James," Amber said sympathetically. "They play on your excitement and urgency, making it harder for you to recognise the red flags. But don't worry, because we will review some general signs that can help you avoid these scams in the future."

"Firstly, pay close attention to the sender's email address," Amber explained, pointing as though she was drawing a list in the air. "Many times, the email will appear to be from a legitimate company, but if you look closely, the domain could be off by a letter or two, or it could be from a free email service rather than the company's actual domain."

Amber added, "Another precaution you can take involves comparing the email sender's domain and the 'reply-to' email domain. For instance, the email could be sent from 'XXX@CompanyA.com', yet the 'reply-to' address might be 'XXX@Freeemail.com'. If these two domains are different, it strongly indicates that the email is a phishing attempt."

"Alright," James replied, "I will pay attention to these tell-tale signs."

"Yes," Amber replied. "Be wary of generic greetings. Most companies, especially those you do business with, will use your name in their emails. If you see a generic greeting like 'Dear customer', that's a red flag."

James nodded again, his eyes revealing he was taking the information seriously.

"Next," Amber continued, "be aware of any emails that urge you to take immediate action. Phishing emails will often try to create a sense of urgency or panic to get you to act without thinking."

She said, "They may claim there's been suspicious activity or too many login attempts, and you must log in immediately, or they might say your account will be closed if you don't act right away."

"And in my case," James added, "they made an irresistible offer, and I was eager to grab it."

"Correct," Amber agreed. "One more aspect to be aware of is the quality of language used. Phishing emails frequently contain spelling or grammatical inaccuracies. So, when you encounter errors in an email, it could be a scam." Amber continued, "However, I foresee this characteristic fading in the future, as cybercriminals could use generative AI to craft eloquent and grammatically correct emails."

"That's quite a bit to remember," James replied, rubbing his temples.

Amber smiled gently at him, "I know it might seem like a lot, and I will put together a checklist[17] for Phishing Scams so you can refer to it until it becomes second nature. The important thing is always to think before you click or respond. If an email seems suspicious, it's best to avoid clicking links or download attachments, and never share personal or financial details unless you're certain the request is legitimate."

Revisiting a previous conversation, Amber stressed its crucial nature, "James, do you recall our discussion about allocating specific time to check emails, ideally on a computer or laptop? There's a greater likelihood of falling into cyber traps when we rush through our emails, particularly on our smartphones. That rule is extremely relevant in this case too." James reciprocated her seriousness with an eager "Understood!"

Amber and James remained on their sofa and shifted the discussion to the diverse world of online scams. Amber, with a touch of serious determination on her face, as she began talking. "There are many types of scams in the market, and I will talk about the more common ones that happen frequently."

"Alright," James acknowledged, understanding the gravity and personal implications of the subject matter.

"Often, we come across the 'Software Update Scam', in which you're alerted that your software is outdated and needs an

---

[17] Go to Appendix 10. Checklist to Protect against Phishing Scams.

urgent update," Amber started. "While it's crucial to keep software updated for security, it's equally important to discern the sources of these notifications." Amber elaborated, "If you're getting notifications via email, encountering pop-ups while surfing the web, or when you stumble on dubious websites mimicking real software firms, or even receive a call from someone alleging to be from a software company's tech support urging an "immediate" software update, these are likely indicators of such a scam."

Deep in thought, James responded, "It's ironic. Cybercriminals exploit our regular software updating practices, which are meant to safeguard us, turning them into a weapon against us." Amber acknowledged, "Exactly right, James! Scammers pay attention to prevailing trends and exploit our behaviour to their advantage."

"Then, we have 'Social Media Impersonation Scams', where someone creates a social media account pretending to be a famous person or brand," Amber continued. "They usually attempt to trick you into sending money, disclosing personal information, or clicking on malicious links."

"What about this 'WhatsApp Takeover Scam' I've heard about?" James asked, looking puzzled.

"Good question," Amber affirmed. "In such scams, a scammer manages to hijack your WhatsApp account and can impersonate you to scam your contacts. They usually do this by tricking you into sharing your six-digit verification code."

James raised an eyebrow, intrigued, "I heard about PayPal email scams?"

"Yes, those are pretty common," Amber explained. "Scammers send fake emails posing as PayPal, asking you to log in via a link they provide in the email to address a potential issue. The site, a clone of the actual PayPal login page, is designed to steal your login credentials."

Amber resumed, "The core concept is identical in the lottery, online purchase, travel insurance, job, investment, loan, and inheritance scams."

James queried, "Is that all?"

Amber explained, "Each scam typically dangles a tempting proposition and then requests money or personal details to deliver the enticing offer."

"And there's also 'Impersonation Scams' which aren't limited to social media. Scammers might pretend to be from a bank, a government agency, or even a relative in need. Then there are rental scams, for rooms, houses, and cars, where a scammer will post a fake rental ad to trick people into sending money or sharing personal information."

"Lastly," Amber concluded, "there's 'Cyber Extortion Scams'. Here, scammers claim to have your sensitive information, like embarrassing photos or videos, and threaten to expose it unless you pay them."

James looked amazed. "Wow, there are so many traps out there."

"True," Amber agreed, "but it's also why we need to be vigilant and informed. Keeping apps updated, not clicking suspicious links, being aware and vigilant, and always verifying sources can drastically reduce your risk of falling for these scams."

After sipping their coffee, James and Amber continued their engaging discussion. "Alright, Amber," James leaned forward, eager to learn. "What does being vigilant entail?"

Looking at James earnestly, Amber began, "First and foremost, it's about staying informed. Cyber threats evolve rapidly, so staying up to date with the latest scams, phishing techniques, and malware is essential."

"Makes sense," James responded, nodding his understanding.

"Second, be wary of any unsolicited communication. This applies to emails, messages, phone calls, and even mail," Amber continued. "Always verify the source before responding, and never give out personal information to unverified sources."

"So, if I get an email from my bank asking for my password, it's most likely a scam?" James asked.

"Correct," Amber replied. "Your bank will never ask for your password. No legitimate company will."

James seemed surprised but quickly moved on, "What else can I do?"

"Be careful with your online presence," Amber advised. "Only share necessary information online and avoid posting about your location, daily routine, or sensitive personal information. This also extends to what information you share on your social media profiles."

"Got it," James replied, "I'll be more mindful of that. Now, I am really looking forward to the online content publishing guide we spoke earlier."

"Good," Amber smiled, "Another important step is regularly reviewing and managing your online accounts. Make sure to check your privacy settings and regularly update your passwords."

"Got it," James said, "And we have already discussed what it takes to generate a strong and unique password."

Amber nodded; glad James brought this up. "You can use a password manager to help remember them. Also, enable two-factor authentication where available."

"Anything else?" James inquired, feeling more and more empowered with each passing minute.

"Yes, dear," Amber nodded, "Always keep your devices and software updated. Updates often include security patches that protect against known vulnerabilities."

Amber added, "There's another crucial step you can take if you suspect you've received a scam and that is, perform a quick Google search. Many scams are used repeatedly, and there's a good chance someone else has already encountered and reported it."

James smiled at Amber, "Alright, I think I can handle all that."

"Of course, James," Amber replied, patting his hand. "Just remember, vigilance is the key. Staying safe online is a continuous effort, not a one-time task."

The atmosphere between them was still light-hearted, but their conversation was serious. The previous incident was a stark reminder of the dangers in the cyber world, making their discussion all the more critical. James vowed that he would take Amber's advice to heart this time.

### *Regularly Review and Delete Unnecessary Applications and Data.*

Amber gauged that there was time for James and her to get through two more subjects before their lunch break. Amber looked at James seriously, "Okay, let's move on to another important topic: reviewing and deleting unnecessary data and uninstalling apps. Have you ever thought about it?"

James sipped his coffee, thinking, "I must admit, I haven't given it much thought."

Amber replied, "It's okay; most people don't. But this is crucial for both data security and privacy. The more data and apps you have, the larger the attack surface for cybercriminals."

James looked curious, "Attack surface?"

Amber noted James' slightly puzzled expression and said, "Let's consider an analogy. Imagine your digital life is a house. Each window, door, or vent can be seen as an entry point. In cybersecurity terms, we call these potential entry points an 'attack surface.' The more doors and windows, the larger the attack surface, and the higher the risk of an intruder breaking in."

James sipped his coffee, deep in thought. "So, the more apps and data I have, the more 'windows' I'm adding to this house?"

"Exactly," Amber confirmed, "And just as you wouldn't leave your doors and windows unlocked, you shouldn't leave your data and apps without security checks either. You must ensure each entry point or app is secure and necessary. If you don't need a window, it's best to brick it up. Similarly, if you're not using an app, it's a good idea to uninstall it."

"That's a great way to put it," James said, the analogy clearing up his confusion. "I never realised how many 'windows' I had open. I'll make sure to close or uninstall the unnecessary ones."

Amber grinned, pleased with his understanding. "And remember, even the windows you need should be strong glass. That's where app permissions come in. Always check and limit what resources an app can access on your device."

"But what about the apps I use regularly?" James asked.

Amber responded, "Even for those apps, reviewing their permissions periodically is important. For instance, a notepad app doesn't need access to your camera or location. If it's asking for such permissions, it's a potential red flag."

James seemed to understand, "That makes sense. And I guess less data means less information that could be stolen?"

"Correct," Amber said, "And not just that, deleting unnecessary data also means less data for you to manage and protect. Plus, it keeps your devices running smoothly."

James seemed convinced, "I'll start doing that from now on. Better be safe than sorry."

Amber smiled, "That's the spirit, James! Remember, cybersecurity is not a one-time activity, but a continuous process."

### *Creating an Individual Breach Recovery Plan*

Amber looked intently at James, her tone taking on a more serious note. "James, the next critical thing we should discuss is an individual breach recovery plan. Have you ever considered having one?"

James looked somewhat bemused, a crease forming between his brows. "Honestly, I have no idea what that is."

Amber pondered before simplifying, " Essentially, it's an outline of what to do during and after a cyberattack. The aim is to limit and control the damage, instil clarity and a sense of calm during panic, and reduce the time required for recovery and associated costs."

James clarifies, "Isn't that something for large companies?"

Amber responded, "Quite the contrary, James. Everyone, and I mean everyone, is susceptible to data breaches, not just companies. Having a recovery response plan helps manage the fallout effectively."

She further explained, "I have helped many compromised individuals, and a common pattern I see is panic and confusion. They panic because they do not know what steps to take. And sometimes, amid the panic, they could do something to worsen the situation further. This plan provides clear guidance and enables victims to respond effectively and calmly."

Seeing the genuine surprise on James' face, she began explaining further, "Let's break it down, James."

"Firstly, we need to know the potential risks and different types of data breaches such as malware, ransomware, phishing, scams and even physical theft of devices that can impact us as individuals. A clear understanding of the assets that we maintain that are of value to cybercriminals will make it easier to identify the type of breach that could happen so that we can pay attention to the signs or indicators of these breaches," said Amber.

"Secondly, identify the accounts affected. Change the passwords of affected accounts, starting with the email account and any accounts with sensitive financial information. Inform the service providers affected by the breach and follow the recommended actions for account recovery." added Amber.

Continuing the discussion, Amber added, "Now, let's address the third step. It's important to determine the extent of the breach and assess if any account login credentials or sensitive personal and financial information have been exposed. After pausing, she continued, "If you suspect it could affect your bank accounts, credit card accounts or any other financial instruments, you must inform your financial institutions, credit card companies, and relevant Law enforcement authorities.

They can advise and help with things like blocking your cards or monitoring your accounts for suspicious activity. You could consider placing a fraud alert or credit freeze to prevent unauthorised access.

Freezing your account is your last resort as it disrupts your digital banking activities."

"Then, you need to purge your system of malware and update your security measures. If necessary, you may need to work with a professional or me," Amber said cheekily. She continued, "To ensure that malware has been removed from your devices. Continue monitoring your accounts and financial statements to watch for signs of identity theft. And at the same time, update your security software, apply the patch as if it is not yet done, change passwords and be vigilant."

"And finally," Amber wrapped up, "it's time for a review and update. Analyse how the breach happened, learn from it, and update your security measures accordingly if you missed out on any security improvements from earlier."

James listened attentively, soaking in the information. "I see, it seems like a lot, but I understand its importance. It's high time I put a plan in place." Amber responded with an encouraging smile, "That's the spirit, James! And remember, detection and prevention are vital, but recovery is just as important. Regularly back up your data, be careful about what you share online and stay updated about current scams and threats. Let's start drafting an Individual Breach Recovery Plan[18] for you."

Amber added, "Just off the top of my head, I was thinking that the personal breach recovery plan can cover the following areas."

- Identified a breach.
- Secure affected accounts.
- Determine the excess of the breach.
- Notify relevant parties.
- Monitor financial statements.
- Purge your system of Malware and Update security measures.
- Educate yourself.
- Back up your recovery.
- Learn from the breach.

Concerned about the amount for James to take in, Amber said, "Okay, James. That's a lot of information we've covered this morning. How about we break for lunch? I'm starving."

---

[18] Go to Appendix 11. Individual Breach Recovery Plan.

James responded, "Sounds good to me. My brain feels full, and my stomach feels empty."

Amber smiled, "That's a good sign, I suppose. It means you've been paying attention!"

James said thoughtfully, "Yeah, I'm beginning to realise just how much I didn't know."

Amber responded, "Awareness! That's the first step towards better cybersecurity. Once you know what you don't know, you can start learning. Remember, it's about creating habits. Once you get the hang of things, it'll feel as natural as scrolling through your social media feeds. Anyway, let's go grab some food."

James said, "I sure hope so. Now, let's go. I could eat a horse!"

Amber, responding cheekily, said, "No horses on the menu, James, but we'll find you something just as satisfying." They both chuckled as they rose from their comfy sofa, closing the chapter on their morning cybersecurity discussion. Lunch and a much-needed break awaited.


### *Pillar 4*
### *Online Behaviour Awareness*

Amber and James indulged in a long lunch break, choosing to feast at a hotel buffet across town from their apartment. After satiating their hunger with a satisfying meal, they returned home. However, Amber was wary that their post-lunch lethargy might interfere with the comprehension of their discussion.

"James," Amber proposed, "I think we should continue our chat at the kitchen table on those high stools. So, we avoid the temptation of a post-lunch nap on our comfortable couch."

Though reluctant, James agreed. "I can't argue with that. My brain feels like it's gone into hibernation already," he joked.

As Amber began brewing a fresh pot of coffee, James took his place at the high stool, awaiting the continuation of their conversation. "We're onto the fourth pillar of your cyber security strategy," Amber commenced, "Once we're through this, we'll embark on the final stage of your journey, which will initiate the beginning of a new ongoing journey."

James looked confused, "Amber, you're speaking in riddles again."

She chuckled and replied, "I guess I am. It keeps things interesting. Adds a sprinkle of mystery to our conversation and your learning journey."

James grinned in response.

"Moving on," Amber continued, "The fourth pillar pertains to your online behaviour. While the previous three pillars mainly addressed safeguarding against cyberattacks infiltrating your digital castle or house, this one is more like a guide to actions to take and avoid while navigating the digital world outside your digital castle or house. Think of it as a set of guidelines highlighting the significance of fostering positive online behaviour and habits to steer clear of the numerous cyber traps on the Internet."

She detailed the areas she intended to address, including:

- Digital footprint awareness privacy settings and data sharing
- Strong password and account security
- Phishing and scam awareness
- Safe browsing
- Digital ethics and responsible social media use
- Software updates and security software
- Data backup
- Account monitoring

James noted some areas were revisited from previous discussions, "We've covered some of these before, haven't we?"

Amber acknowledged, "Yes, we have. Some elements are reiterated in different sections because of their relevance and significance. We won't delve into details on those topics as we have already discussed them extensively."

She then reminded him of the four protective pillars they had discussed: strong and unique passwords, device and network security, data security and privacy management, and online behaviour awareness.

"Consider each pillar as a layer of defence with unique strengths and weaknesses. But when combined, they form a robust cyber defence strategy for individuals."

Amber drew a house analogy to explain the role of each pillar.

"Imagine our cybersecurity as our digital house, James. The first pillar is like keys to our house - complex, unique, and hard to duplicate with two-factor authentication. The second pillar is akin to our home's security systems - alarms, CCTV cameras, and secure locks. It protects our devices and networks from cyber intruders.

The third pillar, data security, is safe in our home, where we secure our valuables. And privacy management is our curtains, determining who sees what. The last pillar, good online behaviour, is akin to our daily routines for our home's safety - like checking doors and not letting in strangers without validation and exercising personal discretion while outside the house to prevent drawing unwanted attention that could jeopardise ourselves or our home."

Through this analogy, James could understand the essence of cybersecurity. He realised the importance of paying attention to every pillar, as it would make their 'digital house' vulnerable.


### *Digital Footprint Awareness*

Amber and James sat at the kitchen table, enjoying their post-lunch coffee. Amber cleared her throat to catch James' attention, who seemed to have drifted off into a coffee-induced reverie.

"James, the first topic under online behaviour awareness is 'Digital Footprint Awareness.' Do you know what that is?" Amber started.

James looked up, his brow furrowing in thought. "I'm guessing it's about the trace, our digital breadcrumbs; we leave online? Like the websites we visit and things we post?"

Amber smiled, impressed with James's recollection from an earlier discussion. "That's exactly right. Every time we use the internet, we leave a trail behind us, known as our digital footprint. This includes our search history, social media posts, likes, comments, uploaded photos, and even the apps we download."

James' eyebrows shot up. "Wow. That sounds extensive. And also, a bit scary. Is there a risk associated with having a large digital footprint?"

Amber nodded empathetically, recalling a client who had encountered the repercussions of having a substantial digital footprint. "I had a client who, like many people, had a significant online presence. As he went about his daily activities, he noticed targeted advertisements on various platforms. It was as if his every move was being monitored and analysed by unseen entities. At first, he brushed it off as a mere coincidence, but then something more troubling occurred.

Out of the blue, he received an email that sent shivers down his spine. The sender claimed to have discovered inappropriate photographs from his past, shared a few in the email, and threatened to expose them unless a hefty sum of money was paid. The client was astounded by the demand's audacity and extremely concerned about the potential harm it might do to his personal and professional reputation. Although a police report was filed, he paid the ransom against the advice of law enforcement. It was a stark reminder of how our digital footprints can be exploited and turned against us in the most unsettling ways."

James nodded, taking in the gravity of what Amber had said. "I see. I hadn't thought about it like that. So, what can I do to reduce my digital footprint?"

Amber appreciated his earnestness and began to outline some steps. "First, regularly check and clean up your social media accounts. Delete old, unused accounts and unnecessary posts or images. Also, control your privacy settings diligently. Secondly, use 'Incognito' or 'Private' browsing modes when surfing the web, as these don't save your browsing history. Additionally, avoid unnecessary online forms or subscriptions which could gather your data."

"Finally, and this is important," she added, "be mindful of what you share online. Always remember, once it's on the internet, it's hard to remove completely."

James looked thoughtful, but a determined edge had crept into his eyes. "I've got some cleanup to do then. Better to be safe than sorry, right?"

Amber smiled, her heart swelling with pride. "Absolutely!! Every step towards safer online habits is a step away from potential cyber threats."

### Privacy Settings and Data Sharing

After discussing digital footprint awareness, Amber moved on to the next topic. "Let's talk about privacy settings and data sharing, James," she said, stirring her coffee.

James looked intrigued. "Okay, what about it?"

"Privacy settings are the controls provided by most websites and apps that allow you to decide who gets to see your information," Amber began, "In most social networking sites, you can customise these settings to ensure that your data is only seen by people you trust."

James interjected, "But I have them set to 'public' because I want to reach as many people as possible."

Amber nodded, acknowledging James' point. "I understand your perspective. When you set everything to 'public,' anyone, including potential cybercriminals, can access your personal information. This puts you at risk for identity theft, manipulation, or scams being conducted in your name.

Adjust your security settings so that your private and personal information remains undisclosed to anyone while allowing your public posts and interactions to be visible to a wider audience. This way, you can continue with your online activities without worrying about your personal information being exposed."

"Oh my, I know we spoke about this earlier, but I did not realise its impact until you just mentioned it," James said, looking concerned, "can you please help me with the adjustments to tighten my privacy setting on my apps? Now, what about data sharing?"

Amber responded, "I will help you tighten your privacy settings." Amber continued, "Now, on data sharing, I know you often collaborate with other creators on your content, right? This means sharing files and ideas online, sometimes sensitive ones."

"Right," James confirmed.

"Well," Amber continued, "When you share data, especially sensitive data, it's crucial to ensure it is secure. Encrypting the data before you send it, using secure file transfer options, and only sharing data with trusted people over secure networks can help ensure that the data doesn't fall into the wrong hands."

James nodded, "That sounds important, but it also sounds like a hassle."

"It may seem that way," Amber conceded, "but not doing so can be even more hassle. If the data is intercepted, it could be misused or even held for ransom. Your creative work could be stolen, or the personal information of you and your associates could be exposed."

James's eyes widened at that. "Amber, can you please explain the steps to take to get started?"

Amber smiled and said, "Of course, James!! Firstly, when sharing files, we must consider how we send them. FTP or File Transfer Protocol can be secure only if implemented correctly. There's SFTP, which stands for Secure File Transfer Protocol, which uses SSH or Secure Shell protocol to ensure data is transferred securely."

James looked puzzled, "Can you explain this again?"

Amber paused, thinking of an analogy, then proceeded, "Sending a file is like mailing a letter. FTP, or File Transfer Protocol, is one way to send a letter, like using a mailbox. But, just like a mailbox, it must be used correctly to keep the letter safe. SFTP is like a locked mailbox - a way to send our letter that uses special tools to keep it safe."

James responded with a smile, "Got it!"

James interjected, "And what about online storage sharing? Like OneDrive, Dropbox or Google Drive?"

"Good question, James," Amber said, "Those platforms can indeed be secure, but again, it depends on how you use them. You must ensure that your accounts have strong passwords and two-factor authentication enabled. Additionally, you should only share files with specific people rather than creating a public link."

James nodded, jotting down some notes, "Okay, got it. I remember we discussed Encryption earlier?"

Amber smiled at his proactiveness, "Encryption is a critical step in secure file sharing. Before you send a file, you should encrypt it. Even if the data is intercepted, it can't be understood without the encryption key."

"But isn't encryption complicated?" James asked, looking worried.

"Not necessarily," Amber assured him. "There are many user-friendly encryption tools available today. It's like putting a lock on the 'envelope' before sending it through the mail. Only the person with the key or the combination can open it up and see what's inside."

James seemed to understand, "I see, so even if someone else gets their hands on it, they can't see the content."

"Exactly," Amber confirmed, "and remember, the most secure way to share a file is to use a combination of these methods: use a secure transfer protocol with a secure platform and encrypt the data before sending."

"That makes sense," James replied, "I'll start implementing these steps. It seems like a small price to pay for ensuring the security of my data and my associates' data."

Amber smiled, satisfied with his understanding, "That's the spirit, James. I'm glad you understand the importance. Good privacy settings and secure data sharing practices are key to protecting your online presence."

### *Strong Password and Account Security*

Amber took a sip of her coffee, looking thoughtful, and then turned to James. "Remember when we discussed creating strong and unique passwords, James?"

James nodded and said, "Of course. It is my first line of defence, and I will change my passwords to strong and unique passwords and use a password manager."

"Great job, James," Amber commended. "Having strong, unique passwords is an essential part of account security. But there's more to it. Now, we need to discuss other account security aspects that will add a layer of protection."

"What else do we need to cover?" James asked, curious.

Amber responded, "Well, remember when we talked about two-factor authentication (2FA)? It's a feature that most online platforms provide. You must confirm your identity in two ways before accessing your account. Usually, it's something you know, like your password, and something you have, like a verification code sent to your phone, and do not share that code with anyone."

James chimed in, "Yes, I remember. I will enable it for all my accounts that offer it, and I will not share the verification code or OTP with anyone."

"Excellent," Amber continued. "Now, let's talk about something we haven't touched on yet: account recovery options. You should set up recovery emails or phone numbers for your accounts. If you ever get locked out, you have a backup way to regain access. It's like having a spare key to your house."

"But what if someone gets a hold of my recovery email or phone number, like what happened to me in my recent compromise?" James questioned her, a hint of worry in his voice.

Amber quickly responded to ease his worry. "That's a good point, James. We also need to secure our recovery email accounts and phone numbers. Use strong passwords and enable 2FA for your recovery email, and for your phone, ensure you have a screen lock and keep it physically secure. It's also like ensuring your spare key is in a secure location."

James asked, "I am unclear what you mean. Can you elaborate on this?"

Amber quickly answered to soothe James' uncertainty, "That's a valid request, James. We must also protect our recovery email accounts and phone numbers. Using solid passwords and enabling 2FA for your recovery email is like keeping your spare house key safe. Also, having a screen lock on your phone and always keeping it close to you is as important as storing your spare key securely. In other words, you don't hide the key under the doormat where anyone could find it; you lock it in a secure box that only you can access."

James nodded, jotting down notes as he said, "I see, so it's all about having layers of security and making sure each layer is as strong as possible."

"Exactly! James," Amber affirmed. "And remember, regularly check your account activity logs, if available. It's like occasionally checking your house for any signs of intrusion. If you see any unfamiliar activity, it's a sign that someone else might have accessed your account."

"I'll keep that in mind," James said, finishing his notes.

Amber smiled pleased and said, "Keep up the good work."

### *Phishing and Scam Awareness*

Amber turned her gaze to James, her tone turning serious. "Now, James, shall we revisit phishing and scam awareness? Do you remember what we discussed previously?"

James, feeling confident, responded, "Absolutely, my dear. Phishing is a scam where cybercriminals try to trick you into giving them your personal information or downloading malware onto your device, often through emails, messages, or deceptive websites. We touched on it while discussing the previous pillar, didn't we?"

"Yes, James, we did," Amber clapped happily, nodding her head with approval. "And it's good to see you recall it. Given that this kind of scam is one of the most common ways cybercriminals target individuals, being aware of it and knowing how to handle it is essential. Can you recall some tips we've shared to stay safe?"

James thought for a moment before responding. "Right; some advice included not clicking on suspicious links or downloading unexpected attachments, being cautious of requests for personal information, and verifying the source of any important communication before responding. Did I get that right?"

Amber was pleased and gave a cheeky grin. "Yes, you did. I'm glad to see you've retained the important points. Does my man deserve a treat tonight?"

James gave Amber a wider grin and asked, "What do you have in mind?"

Amber replied, "I want to buy you a nice dinner tonight."

### *Safe Browsing*

Amber asked James, "Would you like to continue this conversation on our comfy sofa? I think our brains are no longer in our tummy." James immediately responded, "That is a great idea, but please keep the hot coffee coming."

It was a sunny afternoon. Amber could see the condominium swimming pool from their kitchen window, which looked inviting for an afternoon tan and swim. It was something that Amber would do on such an afternoon as today. Instead, Amber was steadfast and went to brew another pot of coffee and continued her conversation with James. "Okay, James, let's talk about safe browsing now. This is another crucial aspect of online behaviour that can significantly reduce your risk of falling prey to cyber threats."

James looked at Amber curiously as she waited for her to finish brewing the hot coffee, "Safe browsing? You mean like not visiting dubious websites?"

"That's part of it, James," Amber replied, smiling at his guess. "But it's not just about avoiding shady websites. Safe browsing includes a range of practices. For instance, ensure your browser is always updated to its latest version. Cybercriminals often exploit vulnerabilities in outdated software, and developers release updates to patch these security holes."

"Ah, I see. So, staying updated helps secure my browser against threats," James replied, jotting another point in his notebook.

"Absolutely. Another important point is to use secure and encrypted connections," Amber continued. "This means looking for 'HTTPS' in the website URL instead of 'HTTP'. The 's' in 'HTTPS' stands for 'secure', meaning the communication between your browser and the website is encrypted and can't be easily intercepted."

"So, 'HTTPS' is like a secure bridge for my data to cross, and 'HTTP' is an open road where anyone can see and grab my data?" James responded, demonstrating that he understood the concept. "You mentioned this earlier, and I have been paying close attention to our discussion." He commented proudly.

"Great! And that's a great way to put it, James," Amber complimented, happy to see him understanding. "Lastly, be mindful of the information you share online, even on seemingly benign websites. Avoid entering personal information unless it's essential and you trust the site."

James nodded in understanding, "It's like not revealing too much about myself to strangers. Got it, Amber. I'll make sure to follow these guidelines for safe browsing." he added, "Do not forget, we need to spend some time over the week to put together my playbook or is it a guidebook for creating my content to maintain its authenticity for my community while without revealing personal information."

Amber responded, "Yes! I remember, and we will spend some time working on that. Speaking of which, we were also follow-up with the social media platforms about the progress on your account recovery." James smiled at Amber and said, "Thanks so much for helping me recover my account."

They paused their discussion as Amber poured freshly brewed coffee into their cups and adjourned the discussion to the comfy sofa in the living room.

Both settled on the sofa. Amber sniffed, sipped her coffee, and continued, "Another part of safe browsing, James, is something many of us tend to forget, logging out of apps when we're done using them."

James looked surprised. "Really? But why? I close the browser when I'm done."

"Well, there are several reasons," Amber responded. "Think of it like locking your car when you leave it. If you don't, someone could easily get in and drive away. It's the same with logging out of apps."

James understood what Amber was saying. "So, not logging out is like leaving my car unlocked?"

Amber confirmed, "Exactly. If you stay logged in, especially on computers that aren't yours, others might be able to get into your accounts. It's like someone stealing from an unlocked car."

James thought about it and sipped his coffee. "You're right. Sometimes, I use the computer at the resort, especially when the Internet connection is faster. But I mostly use my computer. Do I still need to log out, then?"

Amber nodded, "That's a great question, James. Yes, even on your computer, logging off from apps is still important. While the risk is lower than using a shared computer, it's not non-existent."

James was confused. "But it's my computer. How can it be risky?"

Amber smiled at James's question. "It's like your car. Even in your garage, you lock it, right? It's a simple way to keep it safe."

James nodded. "True, but my garage is safe. Why should I worry?"

Amber explained, "What if there was a break-in, James? An unlocked car would be an easy target for car theft or stealing valuables in the car. The same goes for your computer."

James got it now. "It's not about trust but about minimising risk."

Amber agreed, "Exactly, James. Logging out is like locking your car. It's an easy habit that makes things safer."

Amber continued, "Another reason to log out is to protect your information. Many apps, like banking and shopping apps, have sensitive information. Logging out keeps your information safe. It's like not leaving valuables in the car."

James was interested and asked, "Is there more?"

Amber confirmed, "Yes, there is. Logging out also protects against session hijacking. That's when a hacker pretends to be you to get into your account. It's like a thief copying your car key. Logging out makes the copied key useless."

James asked, "Can that happen on my computer too?"

Amber answered, "Good question, James. Let's imagine session hijacking as someone pickpocketing your car keys. Even if you're holding your keys tightly, a skilled thief can still snatch them without realising it."

James was confused. "But Amber, we're talking about my computer at home. How can that happen?"

Amber clarified, "Here's how James. You could accidentally get harmful software on your computer, like malware or a keylogger. This can happen when you click on bad links or download bad files. This bad software can watch what you do or even take over your sessions. That's why it's important to be careful online and ensure your computer is clean."

James understood. "I see. So, even on my computer, there can be risks."

Amber confirmed, "Yes, James. That's why you should always log out. It's like locking your car, even in your garage."

James was surprised. "I didn't know that. Is there more?"

Amber shared, "Just one more thing. Logging out can stop you from accidentally changing things. Like in an email or on social media platforms, a simple click could cause problems. It's like accidentally pressing buttons on your car remote."

 James laughed, saying, "That would be embarrassing. Thanks, Amber. Your car examples helped. I'll make sure to log out of apps from now on."

Amber smiled and said, "I'm glad to hear that, James. Following these steps can make your online activity a lot safer."

***Digital Ethics and Responsible Social Media Use***

Amber and James decided to take a five-minute break. Upon returning, Amber broke the silence with a firm tone: "James, there's another crucial topic we should delve into digital ethics and responsible social media use."

James looked curious and said, "Well, that sounds weighty. Fire away."

Amber began, "Think of digital ethics as the guidebook for the digital game. It guides how we act and make choices in the online realm."

James raised an eyebrow, "Guidebook, huh? I did not know that one existed. Sounds broad. Can you break it down?"

Amber nodded, "Of course, my dear. First, consider privacy. It's about safeguarding personal data, avoiding intrusion into others' online spaces without their approval, and maintaining confidentiality in digital interactions."

James retorted, "So, it's like treating someone's online presence as their home and not barging in uninvited?"

Amber grinned, "Spot on, James. Additionally, we have to respect intellectual property. For instance, we should refrain from downloading or sharing copyrighted content like music, films, images, or text without permission."

James reacted, "But isn't that a common practice, Amber?"

Amber countered firmly, "Common, yes. Ethical, no. It's like stealing someone else's work."

James looked contemplative, "Interesting; I hadn't considered it that way."

Amber continued, "Promoting and sharing accurate information is also our responsibility. We must fact-check before spreading any online content."

James questioned, "Like not spreading rumours without knowing the truth?"

Amber agreed, "Yes! James. We must also encourage respect and kindness online to counter digital bullying."

James looked serious, "So, it's about creating a safe digital environment for all. That makes sense."

Amber concluded, "Lastly, security matters a lot. We need to safeguard our digital spaces against cyber threats. This implies maintaining our systems' and networks' integrity and refraining from harmful practices like hacking."

James looked surprised and firmly said, "Me! Hacking? I will have no part in that, especially with what I have just experienced."

Amber proceeded, "Now let's talk about responsible social media use. It involves respecting others, being authentic, being conscious of your digital footprint, respecting copyright laws, managing your time efficiently, and understanding that your online behaviour can have tangible real-world consequences."

James looked pensive, "Got it. So, our online actions aren't isolated from our real-world identities."

James curiously asked Amber, "Then why is it so difficult to apprehend hackers if online actions are not isolated from real-world identities?"

Surprised at the question, Amber calmly responded, "James, your question is quite thoughtful. The response isn't straightforward, though. In essence, hackers are adept at obscuring their identities and locations, taking advantage of the complexity of jurisdictional boundaries and international law enforcement."

James, with a hint of disappointment in his eyes, acknowledged, "So that's why, just as you highlighted earlier, we must make the task of infiltrating our systems as strenuous, arduous, expensive, and time-consuming as we possibly can by establishing multiple layers of cyber defence for our protection."

Amber nodded, "Precisely, James. Adhering to digital ethics and responsible social media use doesn't just make us better digital citizens, it also substantially reduces the risk of cyber-attacks and adds another layer of protection."

### *Software Updates and Security Software Used*

Amber stood up and stretched, then settled back onto the sofa. She looked at James, "Now, we've already discussed software updates quite extensively, haven't we, James?"

James, displaying a good grasp of their previous conversations, responded, "Yes, we did. I remember that software updates are crucial for maintaining security. They provide patches to vulnerabilities that hackers exploit."

"Exactly," Amber replied, pleasantly surprised by James's clear understanding. "And not only do they fix security vulnerabilities, but they also fix bugs, provide improvements, and sometimes add new features. And you've got to install these updates as soon as possible, right?"

James nodded with a grin, "Yes, precisely. We must never ignore or postpone them because doing so could leave our systems open to attacks."

Amber smiled in appreciation, "That's right, James. I'm glad you've got that point down. Now, let's touch on the use of security software."

James leaned forward, ready to absorb more knowledge, "We've discussed this too, haven't we? But it's always good to review."

Amber agreed, "Yes, security software like antivirus or anti-malware is crucial. They offer real-time protection against various threats and can block or remove malicious software."

James looked thoughtful, "That's like having a guard constantly watching over our digital properties, right?"

Amber smiled and said, "Absolutely, James. The security software continuously monitors our systems, scanning for any potential threats. It can detect and neutralise threats before they cause any damage."

James looked satisfied and said, "So, keep all software, including security software and operating system, updated and use security software to stay safe. That's the key takeaway, isn't it?"

Amber nodded approvingly and said, "Absolutely, James. These are fundamental but vital practices for maintaining digital security. I'm glad you understand their importance."

*Data Backup*

Grinning, Amber leaned forward and said, "Okay, James. We've already covered data backup in some detail. How about you tell me what you remember?"

James, looking confident, started, "Data backup, as I remember, involves making copies of our important data. This way, even if our main device or data source has a problem, we securely store another copy."

Amber nodded approvingly, "That's right, James. And why is this so significant?"

James replied, "Well, backups act like safety nets, right? They shield us from data loss due to hardware failures, accidents, or cyber-attacks. They're our rescue plan if anything unexpected happens."

Impressed, Amber said, "Absolutely, James. And what's the recommended frequency of data backup?"

Feeling confident, James responded, "That would depend on the volume and how often the data changes. But generally, regular backups are critical. For really important data, some even suggest a daily backup, else once a week or fortnight is good enough."

Happy grasping the concept, Amber inquired, "Great! And do you remember the backup strategy we discussed?"

James nodded, "Yes! I remember you mentioned the 3-2-1 backup strategy. It's where we should have at least three copies of our data on two different types of storage media, and one of those copies should be stored offsite."

Amber grinned, pleased with James' retention, "Exactly, James. That's a crucial aspect of data backup. It's like having a spare key for your car in case you lose the original one and keeping it in a separate location to be safe and available when needed."

Amber continued, "You're right. The 3-2-1 strategy is about not putting all your eggs in one basket. By diversifying how you store your backups, you're ensuring that even if one form of storage fails, you still have another option."

James seemed content with the discussion, "Got it, Amber. More backups, diversified storage, and offsite options. This seems like a solid plan to protect our data."

Amber concluded with a smile, "Exactly! You've got the concept perfectly. Data backup, especially following the 3-2-1 strategy, is integral to a comprehensive digital security plan."

### Account Monitoring

As they continued their conversation, Amber turned to James and said, "Now, let's discuss account monitoring, another crucial aspect of cybersecurity."

James raised an eyebrow, "Account monitoring? You mean like checking my bank account?"

Amber chuckled, "Not exactly, James. Account monitoring is more about keeping an eye on your online accounts for any suspicious activities. It's like having a surveillance camera for your digital life."

James nodded, trying to understand, "Oh, I see. So, what kind of activities should I be looking out for?"

Amber explained, "Unusual activities like unexpected password reset emails, unknown devices accessing your account, unrecognisable transactions, or even changes in your account settings that you didn't make. It's similar to spotting unfamiliar faces in your neighbourhood or noticing strange cars parked near your house."

James looked thoughtful, "Okay, I get that. But how can I keep a constant eye on all my accounts? It sounds time-consuming."

Amber acknowledged his concern, "Yes, it might seem like a lot, but it's not as daunting as it sounds. Most platforms offer security features that can help, such as setting up alerts for unusual account activity. I can show you how to set it up later. It's like having a neighbourhood watch. They alert you when something's off."

"But what do I do if I spot something strange?" James asked, slightly worried.

Amber reassured him, "Just like in real life if you see something suspicious, you act on it. You might need to change your passwords, contact your service provider, or, in some cases, alert the authorities. It's like calling the cops when you spot a prowler near your house, ensuring that all your windows and doors are locked, and keeping your valuables safe and out of sight."

James nodded, feeling more confident, "Alright, account monitoring sounds like an important step. It's like being aware of my surroundings in the digital world."

Amber smiled, pleased with James' understanding. "Precisely! In essence, all these practices boil down to online behavioural awareness. It's about being vigilant, just like locking your doors, checking your surroundings, or keeping your valuable belongings safe in the real world. It's a continuous process and forms an important aspect of building a comprehensive cyber security strategy for individuals like yourself."

Amber stood from the sofa and stretched, "Well, James, all this talk of cybersecurity has made me hungry! How about we continue our discussion over a delicious dinner at that famous steakhouse nearby? My treat!"

James raised his eyebrows in surprise, "That sounds great, Amber. But isn't it short notice? Do you think they will have a table available?"

Amber winked, "Don't worry about that. I'll call and see if I can make a reservation."

They both got up from the sofa, placed their coffee mugs into the dishwasher, and moved to change for their evening out. As Amber picked up her phone to call the steakhouse, she couldn't help but glance out the balcony, taking in the beautiful orange hue spreading across the evening sky as the sunset. She dialled the restaurant, and much to their luck, they could get a reservation for two on short notice.

Ready to head out, Amber slipped her hand into James' as they left the apartment. The day's conversation they had, still fresh in his mind, was weighing on James, making him reflect on his online behaviour. He also wondered how his habits and actions in the real world could help improve and strengthen his online security and safeguard his digital identity.

Feeling a touch of paranoia creeping in, he turned to Amber, who sensed his unease. She squeezed his hand reassuringly, reminding him that awareness was the first step towards being cyber secure. And with the tantalising thought of the steak dinner awaiting them, they stepped out into the dusk and took a stroll to the restaurant.

James confessed as they strolled to the restaurant, "Amber, I can't help but feel a little paranoid about all this cyber security stuff."

Amber looked at James thoughtfully, "I understand how you feel. But let me clarify something. The pursuit of cyber safety isn't about paranoia. It's not about living in constant irrational mistrust or fear."

James looked puzzled, "So, what should it be about then?"

Amber smiled, "It's about having a healthy dose of scepticism."

James frowned, "Scepticism?"

Amber continued, "Yes, scepticism. Being critical of information and events prompts us to question them. It's the cornerstone of cyber safety."

James asked, "But how does that work?"

Amber explained, "It's about demanding verifiable evidence before accepting claims. This way, we reduce our susceptibility to manipulation and deception."

James looked thoughtful, "That does make sense."

Amber added, "When signs of a possible cyberattack surface, a sceptical mindset prompts us to investigate further rather than react impulsively due to irrational fear or mistrust."

James nodded, "So it's not paranoia, but scepticism, that is key to maintaining cyber safety."

Amber confirmed, "Exactly! This sceptical mindset, grounded in rationality and evidence-based reasoning, allows us to respond effectively to potential threats and navigate the complexities of the digital world securely."

She said lovingly, "I hope that makes you feel better." As she squeezes his hand during the stroll.

### ***Over To You***

To conclude this chapter, you have learned to view your online presence as a kingdom, implementing stronger passwords, device protections, data privacy, and awareness to safeguard it. Amber's guidance fortified your digital life with practical cybersecurity steps.

In the next Chapter, you'll reflect on your enlightening cybersecurity journey. This Chapter will highlight that cybersecurity requires ongoing learning as technology rapidly evolves. Amber will offer practical tips like newsletters and webinars to stay informed.

# Chapter Four

## Stay Updated and Relevant

With the sizzle of steak and clinking of glasses serving as a gentle background chorus, James looked across the table at Amber and broke the silence, "You know, Amber, reflecting on our discussions over the past three and a half days, it's been enlightening. Cybersecurity, improving my cyber posture. It's a lot to take in."

Amber gave James a warm, loving smile, "It is a lot. But I'm glad you're open to understanding it, James. I am proud of your progress and how far you have come."

Amber stood up from her chair and moved to James' side. She leaned in, planting a tender kiss on his lips. Her whisper flowed into his ear like a soothing breeze, "Take a moment. Enjoy your steak, your wine and our time together."

She gracefully moved back to her seat and reassured him, "When we return to the apartment, we'll wrap up our cybersecurity chat. I promise it will be a lighter topic. We'll focus on how to stay updated and relevant in this ever-changing cyber landscape."

James looked relieved, "I look forward to that." He took a sip of his wine, and his tension visibly lessened. Their dinner continued, filled with a lighter conversation on the next holiday and the shared comfort of their bond.

Back at the apartment, both Amber and James settled comfortably back on the sofa. Amber, with a playful glint in her eyes, began, "So, let's conclude our long and insightful cybersecurity chat. The topic is staying updated on the latest threat developments."

James chuckled, "After these few days, I feel like I should be applying for a job in cyber security."

Amber laughed, "Who knows? You might make a good fit!"

Regaining her composure, she continued, "All jokes aside, the world of cybersecurity is incredibly dynamic. It's crucial to keep up to date with the latest trends, risks and threat intelligence."

James raised his eyebrow, "And how do I do that?"

Amber outlined, "Well, there are several ways. You can subscribe to cybersecurity newsletters, follow trustworthy cybersecurity news sources, follow creditable cybersecurity professionals and influencers, participate in relevant online forums, read books and blogs on cybersecurity, watch training videos or participate in training programme or attend webinars and seminars."

After a pause, Amber added cheekily, "And, of course, you've got your very own live-in cybersecurity expert right here." She playfully poked her chest.

James chuckled, "That's true. I know I can always turn to you for help. And you're all mine!" Then he asked, "Where can I find dependable sources for updates and training to aid my learning?"

Amber took a moment to think before responding, "It's not a simple question, James, but some good places to start are security advisories from banks, government-managed anti-scam websites, law enforcement agencies, the Computer Emergency Readiness Team (CERT) website, and reputable security blogs and news feeds. Some examples are SecurityWeek, SAN Institute, Dark Reading, The Hacker News, and ZDNet Security."

James stood up and lovingly leaned forward to hug Amber tightly.

Amber screamed with laughter and said, "You got that right!" still laughing, Amber said, "Remember, it is important to contextualise cybersecurity to your situation. It is not a one-time deal; it's a lifestyle and should be a daily habit. Just as we take daily measures to ensure our doors are locked."

James nodded in agreement, "You've given me much to think about these past few days."

As they continued their conversation, Amber suddenly grinned at James and said, "You know, James, one of the best ways to learn something deeply is to learn it to teach others."

James raised his eyebrows, "Really?"

Amber nodded, "Yes. When you're learning intending to teach that knowledge to others, you tend to be more thorough in your learning journey. You question more, understand better and remember longer. Just like how you have questioned me throughout this three and half days."

James looked thoughtful, then chuckled, "So, you're saying I might have a new job soon?"

Amber laughed, "Well, not quite a job, but a possible cyber security influencer. Once you've reached a certain level of cyber hygiene and are comfortable discussing cyber security topics, perhaps you could also start helping your friends, especially your creative associates, improve their security postures. You could become a catalyst for change right where you are."

James nodded slowly, "Hmm, that is an idea. I will be James, the travelling cyber security influencer?"

Amber smiled, proud of her man, "I love you, darling." James responded with a kiss on Amber's lips, "I love you too, honey." Amber snuggled up to James, whispering, "Now, let's enjoy the rest of our evening, shall we?"

### *Over To You*

James realises the significance of being cybersecurity savvy as he successfully recovers his social media accounts[19] with the assistance of Amber and his community. Staying secure is an ongoing process and should be an everyday habit. This incident serves as a valuable lesson for James, highlighting the importance of proactively embracing cybersecurity rather than learning

---

[19] Go to Appendix 12. Review the steps Amber used to recover James' social media accounts – 7 Steps for Social Media Account Recovery.

cybersecurity to respond to a breach. Individuals must prioritise cybersecurity regardless of whether they have personally experienced a cyber incident. Since most of you use the Internet and online services daily, taking action and adopting cybersecurity practices to safeguard your digital lives is essential.

Waiting for an unfortunate event to happen is not a practical approach. By proactively embracing cyber hygiene, you can minimise the risks and protect yourself and your digital assets from potential cyber threats.

# # #

# APPENDIX

## Assessments, Cheat Sheets, Tips, Guides and more

Appendix list

1.  A Personal Security Posture Assessment.

2.  Identify, Manage, Organise and Monitor your Digital Assets.

3.  Diagram-3-Step Process to Connect to The Internet.

4.  What is Social Engineering?

5.  What are lookalike domains, and how do we avoid them?

6.  Protect Yourself Against Ransomware Attacks.

7.  Password Checklist.

8.  A Guide to Creating Authentic and Appropriate Cyber-Safe Content.

9.  Be Cyber-Safe on Overseas Holidays and Business Trips.

10. Checklist to Protect against Phishing Scams.

11. Individual Breach Recovery Plan.

12. 7 Steps for Social Media Account Recovery.

13. What are Exploit Kits?


The information in the appendix is a suggested guide to reduce risk and expedite recovery. Since the tactics of cybercriminals are constantly changing, it's crucial to stay informed and adjust these recommendations as needed to maintain their effectiveness.

## Appendix 01

A Personal Security Posture Assessment.


Passwords

1.  Do you use complex and unique passwords for your online accounts?
2.  Do you use at least 12 to 14 mixed characters in your password?
3.  Do you regularly update and change your passwords?
4.  Do you use passphrases?
5.  Are you using a password manager to manage your passwords?
6.  Have you enabled two-factor authentication (2FA) or multi-factor authentication (MFA) for your important accounts? If you have 2FA or MFA, do you share the One-Time Password (OTP) with anyone?
7.  Do you know when your user ID has been compromised?


Device and Network Security

8.  Do you regularly update the application, operating system of your devices?
9.  Do you have an antivirus or anti-malware software installed on all your devices?
10. When utilising public Wi-Fi networks and engaging in sensitive information activities, do you employ a virtual private network (VPN) to secure your internet connection?
11. Do you turn off the Wi-Fi function on your mobile phone when not in use?
12. Are you using WPA3, or at least WPA2 Security on your home network?
13. Do you have a guest network on your home network?

Data and Privacy Management

14. Do you back up your data regularly and have a backup strategy?

15. Do you regularly check the privacy settings of your social media and online accounts?

16. Do you verify that your applications have limited access to only the necessary resources required for their intended functionality?

17. Are you able to recognise phishing or scam?

18. Do you have an Individual Breach Recovery Plan?

19. Do you maintain good data housekeeping habits, such as keeping only active data on your computer and archiving the rest, deleting no longer required data, and so on?


Online Behaviour Awareness:

20. Do you maintain regular housekeeping by deleting unsupported applications or applications you no longer use?

21. Are you mindful about what you post and share online?

22. Do you log off from applications once you finish it?

23. Do you believe you are responsible for your own and others' cybersecurity who are connected to you?

24. Are you cautious about the information you share online and consider its potential consequences on your reputation or personal safety and the reputation and safety of others?

25. Do you practice safe browsing habits like using secure connections (HTTPS) and avoiding unsecured public Wi-Fi networks?

Remember, cybercriminals need to get it right once to compromise you successfully, but you need to ensure that you can detect and prevent cybercriminals from infiltrating all the time.

However, when compromised, a recovery plan is critical to helping you resume your online activities quickly, minimising damages and at the least cost possible. So being aware of your security posture allows you to look at where you need to strengthen.

**Appendix 02**

Identify, Manage, Organise and Monitor your Digital Assets.

1. Identify the types of digital assets:

- Can you identify your digital assets?
- Can you identify which digital assets contain sensitive personal information that needs extra protection?

2. Organise and manage digital assets:

- How do you organise your digital assets?
- Do you have a folder and file naming convention that makes it easy to search and identify?
- Do you regularly assess their relevance and consider archiving or deleting outdated files?

3. Ensure the security of digital assets:

- How do you secure your digital assets? Encryption? Password protection?
- Have you considered the physical security of devices that store your digital assets, such as using secure locks or implementing access controls?

4. Manage user access:

- Do you know who is accessing your digital assets?
- How do you grant access to your digital assets?
- Do you share access with others?

5. Monitor application access:

- Are you aware of the permissions requested by applications accessing your sensitive information and digital assets?
- Have you reviewed and understood each application's privacy settings and access controls?

6. Choose a suitable storage solution:

- What storage solution do you use to store your digital assets? Local storage, external storage, or a cloud storage provider?

7. Establish a backup strategy:

- Do you have a backup strategy in place?
- How often do you back up your digital assets?
- Where are the backups stored?

8. Utilise appropriate tools and software:

- Do you use software or tools to manage and store your digital assets? Such as file synchronisation tools or backup software?

9. Proper disposal of devices:

- How do you dispose of devices that store your digital assets?

By considering and addressing these questions, you can improve the management of your cyber digital assets and ensure their security and longevity.

# Appendix 03

## Diagram- **3-Steps to Connect to the Internet.**

Your devices with applications and data
The user connects  to a Device

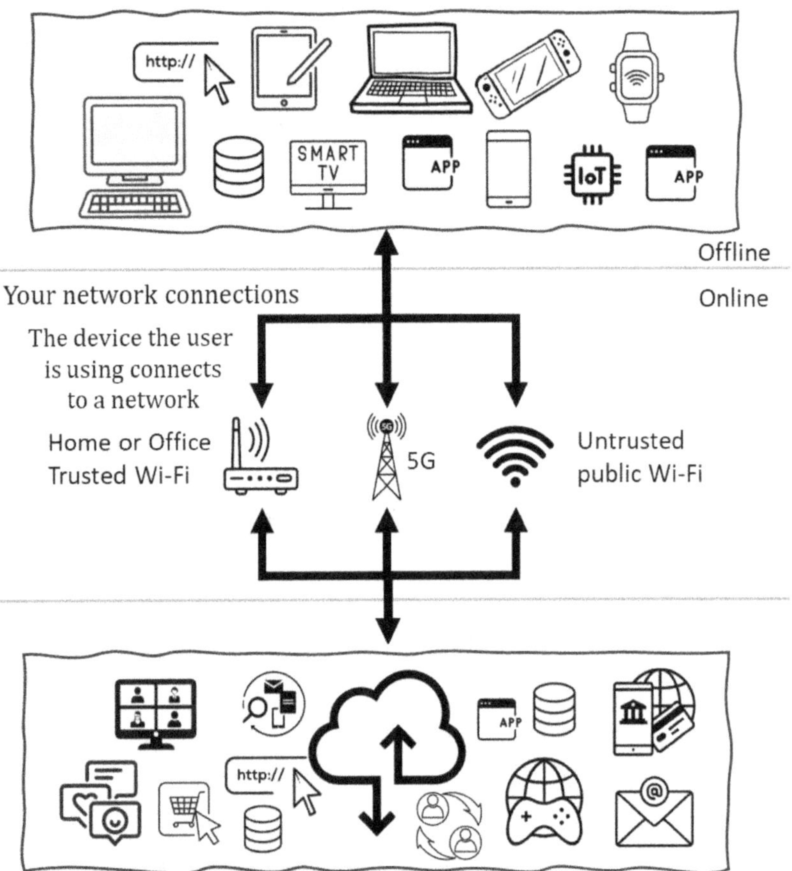


Your cloud or internet connections
To a world of applications and data

The device the user is using connects to
a network that connects to application
and data on the Internet / Cloud

**Appendix 04**

What is Social Engineering?

Social engineering is a sly trick cybercriminal use to charm or deceive individuals into handing over personal or secret information. It's like a digital game of confidence, playing on our instinctive trust in others and our natural urge to assist.

Unlike traditional hacking approaches, social engineering doesn't go after the computers or networks themselves. Instead, it's aimed at the very people who operate those systems.

Picture this: A crafty individual calls an employee, pretending to be from the tech support team and urgently needing specific details to solve a critical issue. This smooth-talking trickster might wheedle out passwords or other guarded information by playing on the employee's desire to be helpful.

The tactics vary and can include the following:
- Cunning emails that look official.
- Hoax phone calls.
- Inventing a whole scenario to lure information from the unwary.

At the core of all these techniques is manipulating human emotions to break down doors that technology alone can't open. This reminds us that the human touch can sometimes be the frail link in our otherwise robust security measures.

Here's a simple analogy to grasp what social engineering is: Think of social engineering as a street magician in a crowded square. You encounter this magician who captivates you with charm and apparent skill, promising a special treat or pleading for your aid in a seemingly harmless task. Little do you know, their real aim is to lead you into a trap, using social signals and human psychology to trick you.

Much like this street magician beguiles you face-to-face, social engineering online tricks you into giving away confidential details or performing actions that breach security, all by taking advantage of human trust and the very nature of social behaviour.

**Appendix 05**

What are lookalike domains, and how do we avoid them?

What is a lookalike domain?

Lookalike domains closely resemble legitimate website domains of well-known organisations or brands, aiming to deceive users by imitating their appearance and structure.

These fraudulent domains have slight variations in spelling, extensions, or subdomains. Attackers use them for phishing, spreading malware, and stealing personal and financial information.

By taking advantage of users' trust, lookalike domains deceive individuals into inadvertently inputting confidential information, exposing them to risks such as identity fraud and other cybercrimes.

Vigilance, verifying website authenticity, checking URLs, and being aware of red flags can minimise the risk of falling victim to such attacks.

Here is an example. The websites on the left are correct; and, on the right, they are a lookalike domain. They look visually similar. The difference between #3 and #4 is harder to tell.

#1 Amazon.com vs Armazon.com

#2 Amazon.com vs Amɑzon.com

#3 Amazon.com vs Amazon.com

#4 Amazon.com vs Amazon.com

Below is a tool to check for Cyrillic, Greek, Coptic and extension characters used in the URL and email exploring the code and block set.

https://apps.timwhitlock.info/unicode/inspect

Most if not all, legitimate URLs, hyperlinks, and email addresses use the normal alphabet and numeric character set consisting of the Basic Latin Block set. So, any deviation from this is a red flag.

10 ways to protect yourself from lookalike domains.

Here are recommended measures that individuals can take to safeguard themselves against falling prey to lookalike domains. Exercising heightened vigilance when visiting websites for file downloads, inputting sensitive personal information, or engaging in financial transactions is crucial.

#1 Double-check URLs.
Before visiting a website, carefully examine the URL to ensure it is spelt correctly and matches the legitimate website you intend to visit. Watch out for subtle variations or misspellings.

#2 Bookmark trusted websites.
Rather than relying on search engines or typing in website addresses, bookmark your frequently visited websites. This reduces the chances of mistyping the URL or landing on a lookalike domain.

#3 Use a password manager.
Most, if not all, of the latest password manager helps users avoid lookalike domains by only auto-filling credentials on the exact websites where they were stored, thereby preventing accidental input on fraudulent, similarly-named sites. It also alerts users if they navigate to a website that isn't on their saved list, highlighting potential risks.

#4 Be cautious of email links.

Avoid clicking links provided in emails, especially from unfamiliar or suspicious sources. Instead, manually type the website URL you wish to visit into your browser or use a trusted bookmark.

#5 Verify email senders.

Check the email sender's address and click on the reply to email address to confirm it matches the company's official email address. If the email address does not match, it is a red flag. Also be wary of emails that claim urgency or require immediate action. This is also a red flag.

#6 Enable email filters.

Set up email or spam filters to help identify and block phishing emails. This can help prevent malicious emails containing lookalike domain links from reaching your inbox.

#7 Use comprehensive security software.

Install reputable antivirus and anti-malware software on your devices. These tools can detect and block access to malicious websites, including lookalike domains.

#8 Stay informed.

Stay updated on the latest phishing techniques and scams by following reliable sources of cybersecurity information. This knowledge will help you recognise potential threats, including lookalike domains.

#9 Educate yourself.

Learn about common red flags and indicators of phishing attempts, such as poor grammar, urgent requests for personal information, or unusual website behaviour. The more you understand phishing techniques, the better you are to spot them.

#10 Report suspicious websites

If you encounter a lookalike domain or suspect a website is fraudulent, report it to the relevant authorities, such as your local law enforcement agency.

This list helps minimise your risk of visiting a lookalike domain.

**Appendix 06**

Protect Yourself against Ransomware Attacks.

Common ways that ransomware is delivered:

- Phishing email
- Exploit kits[20]
- Malvertisement - malicious code in legitimate online advertising networks.
- Social engineering
- Remote Desktop protocol attack - a protocol that allows one computer to access another remotely.
- Software cracks, game modification packs or pirated software.
- Drive-by download - user unintentionally downloads by visiting infected websites, viewing an email, or being deceived into clicking pop-up windows.

Here are some suggested measures that you can use to protect yourself against ransomware attacks.

**Passwords**

- Use Strong, Unique Passwords - Enhances account security and makes it harder for malware to gain access.
- Use two-factor or Multi-Factor Authentication (MFA) - MFA adds an extra layer of security, requiring multiple verification methods.

**Device and Network Security**

- Keep Software Up to Date: Regularly update your operating system, firmware, and applications with the latest security patches.
- Install Reputable Security Software: Use robust antivirus or anti-malware solutions to detect and remove threats.

---

[20] Go to Appendix 13. What are Exploit Kits?

- Enable Automatic Updates: Ensure your software, especially your operating system and antivirus software, are updated automatically.
- Disable Macros and Auto-Run: Disable these features for additional protection.
- Use a VPN: A Virtual Private Network encrypts your internet connection, protecting your data.
- Avoid Public Wi-Fi for Sensitive Activities: These networks often lack robust security, making it easier for data interception.
- Segment Your Network: This divides your network into multiple segments, each requiring unique permissions, limiting ransomware spread.
- Limit User Privileges: Use an administrator account only when necessary and limit the privileges of other user accounts.

**Data and Privacy Management**
- Backup Your Data: Regularly backup your files and data to an external hard drive or cloud storage.
- Regularly Update Your Backup: Keep your backup current to minimise data loss in case of a ransomware attack.

**Online Behaviour**
- Beware of Phishing Emails: Be cautious of unsolicited emails and potential malicious links or attachments.
- Educate Yourself About Ransomware: Understand how it works and the tactics used by cybercriminals.
- Be Wary of Social Engineering Attempts: Be sceptical of unsolicited communication, even if it appears to be from someone familiar.
- Stay Informed About the Latest Threats: Keep up with the latest ransomware variants and tactics.

- Cultivate a Security-Minded attitude: Regular training can help identify potential threats and steps to prevent infection.
- Disconnect from the Network Immediately if You Notice Anything Suspicious: Prevents the ransomware from spreading to other devices.
- Implement an individual Breach Recovery Plan: A clear plan expedites your response to a ransomware attack, mitigating potential damage.
- Consider Using a Browser or Email Filter: Filters can help weed out malicious websites and emails.
- Use an Email Filter: Reduce the chance of ransomware infection by filtering out malicious emails.

If you become a victim of a ransomware attack, these are suggested steps you can take:

1. Isolate the infected device. Disconnect from all networks, Wi-Fi, 5G, wired networks and Bluetooth connections to prevent the ransomware from spreading to other devices.
2. Identify the ransomware, if possible. Cyber security professionals have decrypted some types. So you can regain access to your files without paying the ransom.
3. Report to your local law enforcement agency.
4. Remove the ransomware. Use reputable antivirus or anti-malware to remove the Malware from your system. You may need a separate device to download the antivirus and transfer it to the infected device with a USB drive.
5. When ransomware has been removed, proceed with restoring your files.
6. If you cannot remove the ransomware or restore your files, contact a professional specialising in ransomware removal and data recovery.

7.  Learn from this event and evaluate your security practices. How are you compromised with the ransomware? Was it through a phishing scam? Downloads from a malicious website? Did you click on a link in an email? And so on.

**Appendix 07**

Password Checklist.

1. Avoid weak passwords:
- Do not use default credentials or passwords.
- Avoid using simple and common words found in the dictionary.
- Do not include personal information like your name or date of birth in your password.

2. Use long and complex passwords:
- Opt for passwords with at least 12 to 14 characters.
- Include various character types: uppercase letters, lowercase letters, numbers, and special characters.
- Avoid obvious patterns and sequences: Do not use passwords like "123456" or "qwerty" which are easily guessable.

3. Change default passwords:
- If hardware or software comes with default passwords, change them immediately. Do you do this?

4. Implement two-factor authentication (2FA):
- Do you enable 2FA whenever possible to add an extra layer of security to your accounts?
- If you have 2FA, keep the One-Time Password (OTP) private from everyone.

5. Avoid displaying passwords:
- Do not keep passwords visible on your computer or in any easily accessible location.

6. Do not share passwords:
- Sharing passwords increases the risk of unauthorised access and compromise of your accounts.

7. Use unique passwords for each account:
- Do not use the same password across multiple accounts to reduce the risk of compromise.

8. Use a password manager:
- Use a password manager to securely generate, store, and manage your passwords.
- Password managers can also help you avoid lookalike domains and phishing websites by auto filling your login information only on verified and trusted websites.

9. Set up challenge questions:
- Use challenge questions or security prompts when resetting or changing passwords.

10. Regularly change passwords:
- Periodically update your passwords to ensure continued security. Changing your password every 6 to 9 months is sufficient if you use long and complicated passwords.

Remember, creating strong and secure passwords is essential for protecting your accounts and personal information. By following these guidelines, you can enhance the security of your digital presence and reduce the risk of unauthorised access.

**Appendix 08**

A Guide to Creating Authentic and Appropriate Cyber-Safe Content.

**Do's:**

Content Quality and Authenticity

- Understand Your Audience: Know who they are, their interests, needs, and expectations.
- Create High-Quality Content: Ensure content is accurate, valuable, well-researched and offers insightful information.
- Use Clear and Concise Language: Make your content easy to read and understand.
- Be Authentic: Maintain honesty, transparency, and use your unique voice in your communication.
- Use a Multisource Approach: Ensure your content is accurate and comprehensive by using multiple sources for your research.
- Cite Sources: Always credit the original source when using information or data from other sources.

Content Strategy

- Be Consistent: Regular and consistent posts help maintain your online presence and build a loyal audience.
- Use Relevant Visuals: Use appropriate images, infographics, and videos to enhance your content.
- Engage with Your Audience: Encourage interaction and promptly respond to comments and queries.
- Monitor Performance: Use analytics tools to track your content's performance and guide future content creation.
- Optimise for SEO: Improve visibility by using relevant keywords, structured layout, meta tags, and descriptions.

Privacy, Safety, and Legal Compliance

- Respect Privacy: Do not share personal or sensitive information without consent and adhere to data protection laws.
- Protect Personal Information: Be mindful of revealing personal information that could be misused.
- Secure Your Content: Use strong, unique passwords or passphrases and enable two-factor authentication. Do not share the One-Time Password (OTP) with anyone.
- Be Aware of Scams: Stay vigilant for phishing attempts and suspicious behaviour.
- Comply with Legal Aspects: Respect copyright and privacy laws and avoid defamatory content.
- Follow Platform Guidelines: Adhere to the rules and regulations of each platform to avoid penalties.

**Don'ts:**

Content Strategy and Quality

- Post Too Often: Over-posting can overwhelm your audience and may lead to them tuning out or unfollowing.
- Be Overly Promotional: Balance promotional content with educational, informative, and entertaining content.

Authenticity and Respect

- Spread Misinformation: Fact-check all information before sharing to maintain trustworthiness.
- Post Inappropriate or Offensive Content: Maintain respect and professionalism in all posts.

Privacy and Legal Compliance

- Ignore Copyright Laws: Always get permission to use copyrighted materials and give due credit.

- Share Excessive Personal Information: While authenticity is important, oversharing can put you at risk. Avoid sharing personal information.

Remember, your digital footprint lasts forever, so always think carefully about the content you publish. Following· these guidelines will ensure that you're safe, lawful, and authentic, while also providing valuable content from a variety of sources.

**Appendix 09**

Be Cyber-Safe on an Overseas Holiday.

Before leaving for your trip:

- Update the applications and operating systems to their latest version on all devices.
- Back up all the information on your devices.
- Print out copies of travel documents, vaccination records, and flight and hotel information.
- Install antivirus software and VPNs on your devices.
- Turn on data roaming, and when using public Wi-Fi, use VPN, especially for sensitive transactions, file transfer, or communications.
- Enable screen locks with passwords.
- Ensure all applications have two-factor authentication for account access, where available. Remember to keep the One-Time Password (OTP) private from everyone.
- Bring your own charging cables and a power bank to avoid using public charging stations and cables.

During your trip:

- Turn off Wi-Fi and Bluetooth when not in use to prevent connecting to untrusted or evil twin networks.
- Postpone any application or operating system update notifications until you return home.
- Avoid using geotags on social media, and don't post about your vacation while you're still away.
- Never leave your devices unattended.
- Be mindful of your surroundings while browsing to avoid potential eavesdroppers.

Be Cyber-Safe on Business Trips.

Follow the steps when on holiday with the following additional steps to remain cyber-safe on a work trip.

- Put all the critical files needed for the trip on a separate storage device.

- Use a privacy screen on your computer to prevent prying eyes from viewing your work.

- If you receive an email that appears to be a phishing attempt, forward it to your IT department for investigation.

- Minimise your online time by synchronising emails and data and working on them offline.in other words, do not stay online when you do not need to.

- Most of us would have an out-of-office automated email response. Add a statement asking those who need to contact you urgently to drop you a WhatsApp or Telegram message to arrange a specific time for a discussion. This allows you to maintain the right frame of mind for the call. There is a higher probability of making mistakes when in the wrong frame of mind.

- To ensure your email correspondence's safety, allocating specific time for checking and responding to emails is prudent. And to do them in a conducive environment where you have enough time to do so properly. It is advisable to refrain from checking and responding to emails when rushing from place to place, as the chances of being careless, such as accidentally clicking on hyperlinks or downloading files, are high in these situations.

Remember, these are general guidelines. Depending on your travel destination and itinerary, there might be additional steps you need to take to ensure your online safety while travelling. It's always best to do your research and plan ahead. Safe travels!

Checklist to Protect against Phishing Scam.

1. Check the sender's email address: Many phishing emails appear to come from legitimate companies. Look closely at the domain - it might be off by a letter or two or from a free email service rather than the company's domain.

2. Compare the 'from' and 'reply-to' email domains; for example, if the send and reply emails are different domains, like sent from 'XXX@CompanyA.com', and the 'reply-to' address is 'XXX@Freeemail.com', it's likely a phishing attempt.

3. Beware of unsolicited contact via phone, email, text or social media, especially from an unknown source.

4. Beware of discrepancies in the communication or call that does not seem logical. The scammer may evade your questions or fail to provide credible specifics about the supposed company or offer.

5. Check the quality of the language used: Phishing emails often contain spelling or grammatical errors. If an email has these errors, it could be a scam. However, this will become less obvious as cybercriminals use AI.

6. Beware of irresistible offers: Scammers may play on your excitement to get you to ignore red flags. Always think twice before clicking or responding to an offer that seems too good to be true.

7. Exercise caution when receiving communications from unfamiliar sources that urgently request you to click a link, download a file, or call a number. If it is from a recognised source, it is advisable to call them, using the number from their official website, to verify and clarify the communication, its intent, and the call to action.

8. Beware of software update scams: Be discerning about the source of software update notifications. If the update

comes from an email, a pop-up, a dubious website, or a caller claiming to be tech support, it's likely a scam.

9. Beware of social media impersonation scams: These scams involve someone creating a social media account pretending to be a famous person or brand and tricking you into sending money or disclosing personal information.

10. Beware of WhatsApp takeover scams: These scams involve a scammer hijacking your WhatsApp account and impersonating you to scam your contacts. They do this by tricking you into sharing your six-digit verification code. This method is also used to take over your bank accounts.

11. Beware of PayPal email scams: Scammers send fake emails posing as PayPal, asking you to log in via a link in the email to address a potential issue. The link leads to a clone of the actual PayPal login page designed to steal your credentials.

12. Watch out for impersonation scams: Scammers may pretend to be from a bank, government agency, or a relative in need. They may also use fake rental ads for rooms, houses, and cars to trick people into sending money or sharing personal information.

13. Watch out for cyber extortion scams: These scams involve someone claiming to have your sensitive information and threatening to expose it unless you pay them.

14. Be wary of letters from government agencies, banks, or firms requesting you to undertake unusual tasks, such as settling a fine via a QR code, particularly if you can't remember committing any misdeed. Always call the organisation using the number on their official website for verification. Do this whenever you need to clarify any correspondence.

Websites you can use to determine whether it is a scam.

https://www.scamadviser.com/

https://www.scamalert.sg/

Remember:

The key to avoiding scams is to be vigilant and informed.

- If you suspect a potential scam, conduct a Google search. If others have encountered it and reported it, information should be available online, aiding you in steering clear of it.
- Stay updated with the latest scams, phishing techniques, and malware.
- Be wary of unfamiliar communication and ignore them. But if the response is required, it is advisable to verify and clarify with the source the communication, its intent, and the call to action.
- Lastly, be mindful of the information you share online and on your social media profiles.

Another measure you can adopt is to verify the website addresses mentioned in the communication.

Here are three suggestions to determine if the website is potentially malicious.

1. who.is

Copy the website address.

Visit: https://who.is/ in the search toolbar on the web page.

Look at the "important dates" segment.

Look at the website registration date.

If it is less than one year old,

it COULD mean that it is a malicious website.

2. Scanurl

Copy the website address.

Visit: https://scanurl.net/

Go to the URL field and paste the website address.

This checks websites for Phishing, hosting malware or viruses or websites with poor reputations.

3. Virustotal

Copy the website address.

Visit: https://www.virustotal.com/gui/home/url

This website analyses suspicious files, domains, IPs and URLs to detect malware and other breaches and automatically share them with the security community.

**Appendix 11**

Individual Breach Recovery Plan

A breach recovery plan is a crucial aspect of modern digital life, even for individuals. Here's a simplified 9-step plan.

1. Identify the breach.
- Stay vigilant and be aware of any signs or indicators of a breach, such as unauthorised account activity, suspicious emails, or unusual behaviour on your devices.
- Regularly monitor your accounts and review transaction records for any unauthorised activity.

2. Secure affected accounts.
- Immediately change passwords for compromised accounts, if possible.
- Enable two-factor authentication (2FA) for added security, if possible. And do not share the One-Time Password (OTP) with anyone.
- Contact the respective service providers to report the breach and follow their recommended actions for account recovery.

3. Assess the extent of the breach.
- Determine the scope of the breach by identifying the compromised accounts or systems.
- Check if any sensitive personal or financial information has been exposed.

4. Notify relevant parties.
- If applicable, inform financial institutions or credit card companies about the breach.
- Notify the relevant authorities, such as the local law enforcement agency or the national cybercrime reporting centre, depending on the severity of the breach.

5. Monitor financial statements.

- Keep a close eye on your bank statements for any unusual activity. Monitor your bank statement regularly because sometimes you may not be aware that you have been breached.
- Consider placing a fraud alert or credit freeze on your accounts to prevent unauthorised access.

6. Purge your system and update security measures.

- Purge your system of the Malware or Virus.
- Update your security software and ensure it is running the latest version.
- Regularly apply security patches and updates to your operating system and software applications.
- Use strong and unique passwords for all your accounts.
- Be cautious of suspicious emails, links, and attachments to prevent further compromise.

7. Educate yourself.

- Stay informed about the latest cybersecurity threats and best practices to protect your digital privacy.
- Be aware of common phishing techniques and social engineering tactics cybercriminals use.

8. Backup your data.

- Regularly backup important files and data to a secure and separate location.
- This helps ensure you have a copy of your valuable information in case of a breach or data loss.

9.  Learn from the breach.

- Evaluate the incident and identify any vulnerabilities or weaknesses in your security practises.
- Take steps to improve your cybersecurity measures to prevent future breaches.

Taking immediate action in a security breach is pivotal to curbing its potential harm. Following these steps, you can recover from such a breach and reinforce your cybersecurity protocols to prevent future incidents.

However, it's essential to remember that recovery is as important as detecting and preventing the breach. You can greatly enhance your online security by regularly backing up your data, exercising discretion in sharing information online, and staying abreast of contemporary scams and threats.

**Appendix 12**

7 Steps for Social Media Account Recovery

Step 1: Report the event to the platform.

When you realise your account has been compromised, report it to the social media platform. Most platforms, like Facebook, Instagram, Twitter, etc., have options to report hacked accounts. Ensure you follow the correct procedure to make the report.

It is also the same with accounts that have impersonated you.

Step 2: Gather evidence to prove you are the rightful account owner.

Start collecting any evidence that shows you are the account's real owner. This might include previous emails from the platform, screenshots of your profile, or messages and posts you've made.

Step 3: Follow platform recovery procedures.

Each social media platform will have a unique recovery procedure you must follow. This typically involves answering security questions, providing the email or phone number associated with the account, or verifying your identity via email or text message.

Step 4: Ask friends and followers to help report that your account has been compromised on your behalf.

Getting help from friends can be especially useful if the hacker has blocked your access or changed your account settings. Friends and followers can report suspicious activity or changes on your account, providing additional evidence that it's been compromised.

Step 5: Monitor your account activities.

If you still have access to your account, monitor its activities closely. Look out for unauthorised posts, messages, or changes to your account details. This can also provide evidence that your account has been hacked.

Create a second user account connected to your social media account so that if the account hijackers block you, you can still monitor what is happening via your second user account.

Step 6: Be persistent; follow up with the platform helpdesk but be patient. Be polite.

The recovery process can take some time, and it might be frustrating, but it's important to be persistent. Regularly follow up with the platform's helpdesk to check on the status of your recovery request. However, remember to be patient and polite with the support staff helping you.

Step 7: Learn from this experience.

Once you've recovered your account, take steps to prevent this from happening again. This might include strengthening your password, setting up two-factor authentication, being careful about the links you click, and educating yourself about the latest phishing scams.

Following these steps should help your social media account recovery efforts. Be proactive in protecting your online accounts, but if you find yourself in this unfortunate situation, remember to act quickly and follow these steps.

**Appendix 13**

What are Exploit Kits?

Exploit kits are malicious software packages designed to identify and take advantage of vulnerabilities in computers and networks. They're like a toolkit for cybercriminals, enabling them to break into systems and carry out various malicious activities without the victim's knowledge.

Here's an approachable way to understand what exploit kits are:

Imagine your computer is a house, and this house has various windows, doors, and other potential entry points. Now, these entry points are generally secured. Still, there might be weaknesses or flaws in the locks or construction, known as vulnerabilities.

An exploit kit is like a crafty thief's toolbox. This toolbox is filled with various tools, each designed to exploit a specific weakness in a house's security. The thief (or, in this case, the cybercriminal) roams the neighbourhood (the internet) looking for homes (computers) that have these specific weaknesses. When thieves find a vulnerable house, they use the appropriate tool from their exploit kit to break in.

Once inside, they can steal valuable items (such as personal information), cause damage (like corrupting files), or even take control over the house (or computer).

Exploit kits are often used with other malicious practices, such as phishing or malware distribution. The criminals using these kits keep them updated with the latest tools for exploiting newly discovered vulnerabilities, making them a constantly evolving threat.

Protecting against exploit kits requires keeping software up to date with the latest security patches, using reputable security software, and being mindful of suspicious activity, akin to maintaining robust locks and security systems for a house to keep thieves at bay.


End of appendix

# About The Author

Alvin Rodrigues is a business technologist and cybersecurity advocate with three decades of experience working with global IT companies.

He is an AI enthusiast, provides strategic counsel to executives, and teaches cybersecurity at ESSEC Business School in Singapore. He is an innovative and visionary thinker who can simplify complex ideas and relate them to real-world scenarios.

Alvin appreciates your feedback on this book. Please email him at Alvin@cyfisafe.com with your views.

Alvin writes about cybersecurity on his LinkedIn page regularly. Connect with him via this LinkedIn QR code to read his posts.

Alternatively, visit him at URL https://www.linkedin.com/in/alvinsrodrigues/ to connect.

www.ingramcontent.com/pod-product-compliance
Lightning Source LLC
Chambersburg PA
CBHW071613150726
48000CB00004B/1704